family circle®

The Tastes of
Christmas

The Family Circle® Promise of Success

Welcome to the world of Confident Cooking,
created for you in the Australian **Family Circle®
Test Kitchen,** where recipes are double-tested by
our team of home economists to achieve a
high standard of success—and delicious
results every time.

MURDOCH BOOKS®
Sydney • London • Vancouver • New York

C O N T E

Sugar-free pudding, page 52

Salmon and fennel frittata, page 81

Berries in Champagne jelly, page 59

Pickled prawns, page 36

N T S

HONEY-GLAZED HAM, page 12

PINEAPPLE AND MANGO JAM, page 94

The Publisher thanks the following for their assistance: Chief Australia, Sunbeam Corporation, Kambrook, Sheldon & Hammond, Southcorp Appliances, Bertoli Olive Oil, Waterford Wedgewood, Christoflé, Villeroy & Boch, Hale Imports, Ruby Star Traders, Camarge.
Front cover: Steamed Christmas pudding (page 48)
Inside front cover: Ginger pecan biscotti (page 103)
Back cover: Roast turkey (page 10)

PORK WITH APPLE AND PRUNE STUFFING, page 18

All recipes are double-tested by our team of home economists. When we test our recipes, we rate them for ease of preparation. The following cookery ratings are on the recipes in this book, making them easy to use and understand.

A single Cooking with Confidence symbol indicates a recipe that is simple and generally quick to make—perfect for beginners.

Two symbols indicate the need for just a little more care and a little more time.

Three symbols indicate special dishes that need more investment in time, care and patience—but the results are worth it.

IMPORTANT
Those who might be at risk from the effects of salmonella food poisoning (the elderly, pregnant women, young children and those suffering from immune deficiency diseases) should consult their GP with any concerns about eating raw eggs.

CHRISTMAS DAY COUNTDOWN

CHRISTMAS is a time of relaxing with family and friends, of giving and receiving, and indulging in the better things in life. However, if you're the one doing all the organising, it can all seem a bit overwhelming. We are trying to take some of the pressure off, to help you plan ahead and save time and worry, whether your event be quiet pre-Christmas drinks or a fully fledged Christmas day extravaganza. After all, you should be able to relax and enjoy the spirit of the season with everyone else. The key to success is organisation, so here's a schedule to help you along.

1 YEAR AHEAD

* Of course, it sounds ridiculous to start planning this early, but the post-Christmas sales are an ideal time to stock up on budget-priced decorations and place settings.

3 MONTHS AHEAD

* Work out your budget, a rough guest list and plan your menu.
* If you need to hire equipment—anything from a marquee to cutlery—do so.
* Christmas cakes and puddings can be made well ahead of time if stored properly. Wrap securely in greaseproof paper, then in plastic wrap and store in an airtight container in the refrigerator or a cool, dark place. Indeed, a long storage time is actually beneficial as it allows the flavours to develop. As a general rule, Christmas cake can be stored for up to 3 months and puddings for up to 6 weeks. Both can also be frozen for up to 12 months.
* Make your liqueur fruits so they are ready for Christmas day or for giving as gifts. If you can, buy fruits in season when they are cheaper and full of flavour as they will keep bottled for up to 6 months.

1 MONTH AHEAD

* If you have storage space, purchase wine, beer and soft drinks now. Or, if you have planned a large party, order drinks now and have them delivered on the day.
* Order turkeys and hams. As a general guide a 7 kg ham will serve around 20 people and a 4.5 kg turkey will feed 6–8 people when served as a main course with vegetables and all the trimmings.

1 WEEK AHEAD

* Ensure you have a carving knife and fork on hand—it is a good idea to have your knives professionally sharpened. Some sturdy chopping boards will come in handy too! Make sure your baking dish is large enough for your ham or turkey.
* Prepare your shopping list and buy most of your non-perishable ingredients. Pick up items like napkins, tablecloths, candles and toothpicks while you are shopping.
* Make your gingerbread house, mince pies, shortbread, biscotti, panettone, panforte, stollen, etc and keep them well sealed in an airtight container.

❋ Ice the Christmas cake, if required (see page 64).
❋ Make your jams, curds, chocolates and fudges.
❋ Freeze ahead—the great thing about many Christmas goodies is that they can be made ahead and either frozen or left, well sealed, at either room temperature or in the refrigerator until ready to use.

2 DAYS AHEAD

❋ Try to choose a dessert, starter or side dish that can be made, at least partially, beforehand and will keep refrigerated.
❋ If you are having a buffet, wrap the cutlery in napkins and place in an attractive, decorated basket.
❋ Think about the food you are serving and select your serving dishes, platters and utensils. Make sure they are all clean, polished and a suitable size.
❋ Fill up your salt and pepper shakers, sugar bowls, etc.
❋ Defrost anything that needs defrosting. A large turkey can take up to 3 days—take it out of the original packaging and sit it on a rack in a baking tray in the refrigerator. Make sure it is not sitting in the liquid while thawing. Cover with clean plastic wrap.

1 DAY AHEAD

❋ Set your table—iron the tablecloth, put the candles in holders, fold the napkins and lay out any decorations.
❋ Polish glasses and cutlery, and then put a light cloth over the whole setting to ensure no dust or greasy fingers spoil your hard work.
❋ Buy all your last-minute fresh produce, seafood and fresh flowers.
❋ Make stuffings and refrigerate them in a covered bowl.
❋ Make your pavlova, or any dessert sauces or custards that will keep overnight.
❋ Prepare the glaze for your ham and score and stud the ham with cloves.
❋ Refrigerate all your drinks now unless you are purchasing ice tomorrow.
❋ Don't forget the little things like butter, coffee, milk and garbage bags.
❋ Calculate how long things will take to cook and plan what to cook when.

Christmas Day

❋ Preheat your oven. Just prior to cooking, prepare your roast by trimming, trussing, tying or stuffing as required. Do not stuff a turkey ahead of time as bacteria can develop in the cavity even when refrigerated and no-one wants to be responsible for giving their entire family food poisoning—especially on Christmas day!!
❋ Put the ham, turkey or other roast on to cook.
❋ Vegetables to be roasted should go on an hour before the meat is cooked.
❋ Other vegetables should be peeled and chopped when you first put your roast on and finished off just toward the end of cooking. Vegetables that don't take long to cook, such as peas, beans or asparagus, should be cooked while your roast is resting.
❋ Gravy can also be made while the meat is resting.
❋ If you are having pudding, it will take 2 hours to reheat.
❋ Remember to chill the drinks, warm the plates, put on some music, fill your glass and, above all, enjoy yourself!

HOW TO CARVE A ROAST

Carving a roast can be tricky, so follow these instructions and even the most inexperienced carver will be able to serve a perfect Christmas roast in a quick and fuss-free manner.

TURKEY AND ham are the most popular Christmas roasts—and the most daunting. They are rarely eaten at other times of the year and can easily confound even the most confident of cooks when it comes to carving and presenting them.

Before carving any roast, it is important to let the meat 'rest' for 15 minutes or so. Remove the roast from the oven and cover it with foil so the heat does not escape too quickly and the juices can settle and distribute evenly, moistening and tenderising the flesh.

Also, make sure your carving knife is sharp and try to slice rather than saw—the more you hack into the meat, tearing the flesh, the more juices are lost, making the meat dry and tasteless. An electric knife can make life much easier. A carving fork is also important for holding the meat steady. Do not pierce the meat if possible—try to use the back or the flat of the fork to get a good hold. When carving a bird, however, a sharp-pronged fork is usually needed to dig deep into the carcass (not the flesh) to keep it still.

Always carve on a carving board, not a serving platter. China and metal surfaces can scratch easily and can be quite slippery, causing you to lose control of the knife.

It is preferable to use a carving board with a rim around the edges to catch any excess juices—this not only stops the juices from spilling over onto the table but it also means they can be strained off and used in your gravy for an extra boost of flavour. It is also a good idea to place a damp cloth underneath your board to keep it steady while carving.

Cut a slice from the underside of the ham to steady it while carving.

Cut thin slices, working away from the knuckle.

Remove a wedge of ham from the knuckle end before you carve.

Cut the slices away from the bone and serve.

Remove the leg and thigh section from the body of the turkey.

Similarly, remove the turkey wing by cutting through the joint.

With larger birds it is possible to separate the leg and thigh.

Carve the turkey breast, using the fork to keep the bird steady.

HAM

1 After resting, place the ham on a cutting board with the bone to the left. Use a clean tea towel to hold the bone firmly while carving. Remember to keep your fingers away from the blade! Slice a piece from the underside of the leg so that it sits flat on the board. Remove this slice and set aside.

2 Slice into the meat about 10 cm from the knuckle. Make another cut at an angle to the first so that it forms a wedge, then remove. Continue cutting to the right, cutting several thin slices right down to the bone. The meat will still be attached to the bone so to release the pieces you must run the knife along the bone, under the meat. Lift off the slices with the flat of the knife. Cut enough slices for serving, covering the slices with foil as you go if the ham is to be served warm.

TURKEY

1 After resting, place the turkey on a cutting board, breast-side-up and with the legs facing you.

2 Use a carving fork to steady the bird and cut downward into the skin and meat where the leg meets the breast. Bend the leg outwards with the carving knife until you can see the joint where the thighbone and the backbone connect. Keep cutting at a slight angle towards the joint, then cut down and through it until the leg section (the thigh and drumstick) can be easily removed. Depending on the size of the turkey, you can also cut through the leg at the joint to remove the thigh and have two separate pieces. Set the meat aside on a warm serving dish and keep covered with foil while you are carving the rest of the turkey. This will keep it warm and stop it from drying out.

3 On the same side of the bird, find where the wing meets the body and cut down, again until you meet the joint. You may need to pull the wing out with your left hand while you are cutting with your right hand to loosen the wing from the bird. Set aside and cover to keep warm.

4 Continuing on the same side, begin to carve the breast. Start at the top of the breast where it attaches to the ridge of bone and carve downwards in even slices, at a slight angle, towards the cutting board. Add to the rest of meat and cover. Now repeat this process on the other side of the turkey. To remove the wishbone, snip the sinews on either side.

5 Remove the stuffing from the opening of the carcass with a spoon and, depending on the texture of the stuffing, serve it either in slices or in spoonfuls.

CHRISTMAS DAY

CHRISTMAS DAY is a time of family and friends, of indulging in fine foods and celebrating all there is to be grateful for. It's also a chance to get out your best tableware. . . Fine china plates, crystal glassware and thick damask tablecloths— a traditional Christmas table setting can't help but invoke the holiday spirit. How could you eat roast turkey any other way?

ROAST TURKEY

Christmas dinner would hardly seem complete without an enormous turkey, with stuffing and roast vegetables, weighing down the centre of the table. Make gravy to accompany it, and why not try bread sauce or some cranberry relish as well.

Preparation time: 45 minutes
Total cooking time: 2 hours +
    15 minutes resting
Serves 6–8

4.5 kg turkey
stuffing (see pages 20–21)
2 tablespoons oil
1/2 cup (125 ml) chicken stock

1 Preheat the oven to moderate 180°C (350°F/Gas 4).

2 Remove the neck and giblets from inside the turkey. Wash the turkey well and pat the cavity and the skin dry with paper towels.

3 Spoon the stuffing loosely into the turkey cavity. Tuck the wings underneath and join the cavity with a skewer. Tie the legs together. Place on a rack in a baking dish. Roast for 2 hours, basting with the combined oil and the chicken stock. Cover the breast and legs with foil after 1 hour if the turkey is overbrowning. Test by inserting a skewer between the drumstick and thigh. If the turkey is cooked, the juices will run clear. Reserve any pan juices for making the gravy. Cover and leave to rest for 15 minutes before carving.

NUTRITION PER SERVE (8)
Protein 125 g; Fat 22 g; Carbohydrate 0 g; Dietary Fibre 0 g; Cholesterol 275 mg; 2931 kJ (701 cal)

NOTE: It is always a good idea to salt the turkey as a precaution against the growth of harmful bacteria. To do this, pour 2 tablespoons salt into the turkey carcass. Use your hand, or a clean tea towel, to rub the salt into the carcass, making sure it covers all of the inside. Rinse the carcass with water, making sure all the salt is removed. Pat dry with another clean tea towel and proceed with stuffing and baking the turkey.

Remove the neck and the giblets from inside the turkey before you roast it.

After stuffing the turkey, tuck the wings underneath the body.

TURKEY GRAVY

Once the turkey is cooked, drain off all except 2 tablespoons of the pan juices from the baking dish. Place the dish on the stove over low heat, add 2 tablespoons plain flour and stir over medium heat until well browned. Gradually add 1½ cups (375 ml) hot chicken stock, stirring until the gravy boils and thickens. *Makes 1¼ cups (315 ml)*

BREAD SAUCE

Push 2 whole cloves into an onion and place it in a pan with 1 cup (250 ml) milk and a bay leaf. Bring to the boil, watching carefully so that it does not boil over, then remove from the heat, and leave for 10 minutes. Remove the onion and bay leaf and discard. Add 50 g breadcrumbs (made with about 3 slices of day-old bread in a food processor) to the pan and season with salt and freshly ground black pepper. Return to the heat, cover and simmer gently for 10 minutes, stirring occasionally. Stir in 3 tablespoons cream. *Makes 1 cup (250 ml)*

CRANBERRY RELISH

Put 4 cups (500 g) fresh or frozen cranberries, ½ cup (125 g) sugar, ½ cup (125 ml) fresh or bottled orange juice, the rind of 1 medium orange, 1 cinnamon stick and 2 tablespoons port in a heavy-based pan. Bring to the boil, then reduce the heat and simmer for 5 minutes. Remove the cinnamon stick, making sure you remove any small pieces that have broken away from the stick, and orange rind and cool before serving. Store, covered, in the refrigerator for up to a week. *Makes 2 cups (500 ml)*

Join the cavity with a skewer and tie the legs together to seal the stuffing in.

Place the turkey on a rack in a baking dish to roast.

12

HONEY-GLAZED HAM

A mustard and redcurrant glaze is a delicious alternative to this honey glaze, and either can be accompanied by cumberland or mustard sauce.

Preparation time: 30 minutes
Total cooking time: 65 minutes +
   15 minutes resting
Serves 20

7 kg leg ham
cloves, to garnish

GLAZE
⅔ cup (125 g) soft brown sugar
¼ cup (90 g) honey
1 tablespoon English mustard

1 Preheat the oven to moderate 180°C (350°F/Gas 4). Using a sharp knife, cut through the rind 6 cm from the shank end. To remove the rind from the ham, run a thumb around the edge, under the rind and carefully pull back. Using a sharp knife, remove and discard some of the excess fat from the ham.

2 Using a sharp knife, score the fat with cuts crossways and then diagonally to form a diamond pattern. Do not cut all the way through to the ham or the fat will fall off during cooking. Press a clove into the centre of each diamond.

3 To make the glaze, combine all the ingredients in a bowl and spread carefully over the ham with a palette knife or the back of a spoon.

4 Place the ham on a rack in a deep baking dish. Add 2 cups (500 ml) water to the dish. Cover the ham and dish securely with foil, and cook for 45 minutes.

5 Remove the ham from the oven. Increase the heat to hot 210°C (415°F/Gas 6–7). Return the ham to the oven and bake for 20 minutes, or until the surface is slightly caramelised. Rest for 15 minutes before carving.

NUTRITION PER SERVE
Protein 53 g; Fat 10 g; Carbohydrate 10 g; Dietary Fibre 0 g; Cholesterol 144 mg; 1439 kJ (345 cal)

Use a sharp knife to cut through the rind at the shank end of the ham.

Run your thumb under the rind and carefully pull it back.

13

Score the ham in a diamond pattern using a sharp knife.

Press cloves into the diamonds and cover the ham with the glaze.

CUMBERLAND SAUCE

Boil the shredded rind of 2 oranges and 1 lemon with 1 cup (250 ml) water for 5 minutes, then drain and set aside. Squeeze the juice from the oranges and lemon and place in a pan. Add a 225 g jar redcurrant jelly, 2 teaspoons Dijon mustard, 2 tablespoons red wine vinegar, 1 cup (250 ml) port and the reserved rind. Slowly bring to the boil, stirring as the jelly melts. Reduce the heat and simmer for 15 minutes. Season and serve at room temperature. Cover and refrigerate for up to 1 week. *Makes 2 cups (500 ml)*

MUSTARD CREAM

Combine 1/3 cup (90 g) French or grain mustard, 2 crushed garlic cloves, 1 cup (250 g) sour cream and 1/2 cup (125 ml) cream. Leave, covered, in the refrigerator for 1 hour then season well before serving. This sauce can be served warm by placing it in a small pan and stirring over low heat until heated through. Take care not to boil the sauce or it will split. *Makes 2 cups (500 ml)*

MUSTARD AND REDCURRANT GLAZE

Combine 1/3 cup (90 g) Dijon mustard, 1 cup (315 g) redcurrant jelly, 4 crushed garlic cloves, 2 tablespoons oil and 2 tablespoons soy sauce in a pan. Stir over medium heat until the jelly has melted. Take care that the glaze does not catch on the bottom of the pan. Use to glaze ham in the same way as the honey glaze is used. *Makes 1 1/3 cups (330 ml)*

ROAST BEEF WITH YORKSHIRE PUDDINGS

Cooking times for roast beef vary, but as a general rule, for a rare result, cook for 20 minutes per 500 g, for a medium result, cook for 30 minutes per 500 g, and for a well-done result, cook for 35 minutes per 500 g.

Preparation time: 15 minutes +
    1 hour standing
Total cooking time:
    1 hour 40 minutes +
    15 minutes resting
Serves 6

2 kg piece roasting beef
    (Scotch fillet, rump or sirloin)
2 cloves garlic, crushed

YORKSHIRE PUDDINGS
¾ cup (90 g) plain flour
½ cup (125 ml) milk
2 eggs

1 Preheat the oven to very hot 240°C (475°F/Gas 9). Rub the beef with the garlic and some freshly cracked black pepper and drizzle with a little oil. Place on a rack in a baking dish and roast for 20 minutes.

2 Meanwhile, to make the Yorkshire puddings, sift the flour and ½ teaspoon salt into a large bowl, make a well in the centre and whisk in the milk. In a separate bowl, whisk the eggs until fluffy, then add them to the batter and mix well. Add ½ cup (125 ml) water and whisk until large bubbles form on the surface. Cover the bowl with plastic wrap and refrigerate for 1 hour.

3 Reduce the heat to moderate 180°C (350°F/Gas 4) and roast the meat for 1 hour for a rare result, or longer for well done. Cover loosely with foil and leave in a warm place for 20 minutes before carving. Increase the oven to hot 220°C (425°F/Gas 7).

4 Pour off all the pan juices into a jug and reserve for making gravy. Put ½ teaspoon of the juices into 12 ⅓ cup (80 ml) muffin tins. Take the batter out of the refrigerator and

whisk again until bubbles form on the surface. Pour the batter into each muffin tin to three-quarters full. Place in the oven and cook for

20 minutes, then reduce the oven to moderate 180°C (350°F/Gas 4) and cook for a further 10 minutes, or until puffed and lightly golden.

Rub the beef with crushed garlic and freshly cracked black pepper.

Whisk the ingredients for the Yorkshire puddings to a smooth batter.

CREAMY HORSERADISH

Combine 175 g horseradish cream, 1 finely chopped spring onion bulb and 1/4 cup (60 g) sour cream in a small bowl. Fold in 1/2 cup (125 ml) softly whipped cream. Season. *Makes about 1 1/2 cups (375 ml)*

RED WINE GRAVY

Place 2 tablespoons of reserved pan juices in the baking dish on the stove over low heat. Add 2 tablespoons plain flour and stir well, ensuring that you scrape the bottom of the dish to incorporate all the sediment. Cook over medium heat for 1–2 minutes, stirring constantly, until the flour is well browned. Combine 1/3 cup (80 ml) red wine and 2 1/2 cups (600 ml) beef stock, and gradually stir into the flour mixture, making sure the liquid is well absorbed before each addition. Heat, stirring constantly, until the gravy boils and thickens. Simmer for 3 minutes, then season to taste with salt and black pepper. *Makes 3 cups (750 ml)*

BEARNAISE SAUCE

Put 3 chopped spring onions, 1/2 cup (125 ml) dry white wine, 2 tablespoons tarragon vinegar and 1 tablespoon chopped fresh tarragon (or 1 teaspoon dried tarragon) in a pan and boil rapidly until only 2 tablespoons of liquid is left. Strain with a fine sieve, put in a food processor with 4 egg yolks and process for 30 seconds. With the motor running, slowly add 125 g melted butter in a thin stream. Process until the sauce has thickened and is a smooth consistency. Add 1 tablespoon lemon juice, and season with salt and white pepper. *Makes 1 cup (250 ml)*

Make the gravy and carve the roast while the puddings are baking.

5 Serve the roast beef with the hot Yorkshire puddings and gravy.

NUTRITION PER SERVE
Protein 100 g; Fat 33 g; Carbohydrate 35 g; Dietary Fibre 2 g; Cholesterol 430 mg; 3510 kJ (840 cal)

Put 1 teaspoon of pan juices in each patty pan before adding the batter.

Bake the puddings for 10 minutes, or until they are risen, crisp and golden.

ROAST DUCK

Roast duck is a delicious alternative to turkey. Make sure the duck is sitting on a roasting rack in the baking dish while cooking to drain off excess fat.

Preparation time: 40 minutes
Total cooking time:
    2 hours 15 minutes +
    15 minutes resting
Serves 4

2 kg duck, with neck
2 chicken wings, chopped
1/2 cup (125 ml) white wine
1 onion, chopped
1 small carrot, sliced
1 tomato, chopped
bouquet garni (a bay leaf and
    small sprigs of parsley,
    thyme and marjoram,
    in muslin tied with string)

1 Place the duck neck, chicken wings and wine in a pan. Simmer over medium heat for 5 minutes, or until the wine has reduced by half. Add the onion, carrot, tomato, bouquet garni and 2 cups (500 ml) water. Bring to the boil and simmer gently for 40 minutes. Strain and set aside about 1 cup (250 ml) of the stock. Discard the vegetables and the bouquet garni.

2 Preheat the oven to moderate 180°C (350°F/Gas 4). Place the duck in a large pan, cover with boiling water, and then drain. Dry with paper towels. Using a fine skewer, prick all over the outside of the duck, piercing only the skin, not the flesh. Place the duck breast-side-down on a roasting rack in a baking dish and roast for 50 minutes.

3 Drain off any fat, turn the duck over and add the stock to the pan. Roast for 40 minutes, or until the breast is golden brown. Pour off and reserve the stock. Remove the duck from the pan and leave in a warm place for 15 minutes before carving. Reserve any pan juices for making gravy or orange sauce.

NUTRITION PER SERVE
Protein 90 g; Fat 30 g; Carbohydrate 3 g; Dietary Fibre 1.5 g; Cholesterol 550 mg; 2689 kJ (640 cal)

Make a bouquet garni with a bay leaf and sprigs of parsley, thyme and marjoram.

After simmering the stock ingredients, strain and reserve 1 cup of the liquid.

ORANGE SAUCE

Skim any extra fat off the reserved stock from the duck. Add 2 tablespoons shredded orange rind, 2/3 cup (170 ml) orange juice and 1/3 cup (80 ml) Cointreau. Bring to the boil, then reduce the heat and simmer gently for 5 minutes. Blend 2 teaspoons cornflour with 1 tablespoon water, and stir into the sauce until it boils and thickens. *Makes 2/3 cup (170 ml)*

CHERRY SAUCE

Drain 350 g morello (sour) cherries, reserving the syrup. Measure the syrup and add red wine to make 1 cup (250 ml). Combine the syrup and wine in a pan with 1 strip orange rind, 1 table-spoon sugar, 1/2 small chicken stock cube, and 1/4 teaspoon ground cinnamon. Bring to the boil, then reduce the heat and simmer for 4 minutes. Blend 2 teaspoons cornflour with 1 tablespoon water and stir into the sauce. Return to the boil, stirring, until thickened. Add the cherries and simmer for 5 minutes. Remove the rind, add 15 g butter, stir until melted and serve. *Makes 1 1/2 cups (375 ml)*

DUCK GRAVY

Strain the juices from the baking dish into a small jug. Discard all but 1 tablespoon of the fat from the surface of the juices. Place the reserved fat in a pan over medium heat, add 2 tablespoons plain flour and stir until smooth. Cook over moderate heat for 3–4 minutes, or until lightly golden. Remove from the heat and add the remaining pan juices and 1 cup (250 ml) chicken stock, stirring until combined. Return to the heat and cook, stirring, until the gravy thickens. *Makes 1 cup (250 ml)*

Use a fine skewer to prick the skin of the duck, being careful not to pierce the flesh.

Remove any fat from the pan, turn the duck over and pour the stock into the pan.

PORK WITH APPLE AND PRUNE STUFFING

Pork rind must be scored before cooking for it to crisp up properly. Ask your butcher to do this for you.

Preparation time: 35 minutes
Total cooking time:
 2 hours 15 minutes +
 15 minutes resting
Serves 8

2 kg piece boned pork loin
1 small green apple, chopped
1/3 cup (90 g) pitted chopped
 prunes
2 tablespoons port
1 tablespoon chopped fresh parsley
olive oil and salt, to rub on pork

1 Preheat the oven to very hot 240°C (475°F/Gas 9). Score the pork rind (if the butcher hasn't already done so). To make the stuffing, combine the apple, prunes, port and parsley. Lay the pork loin fat-side-down on a board. Spread the stuffing over the meat side, roll up and secure with skewers or string at regular intervals. If some of the filling falls out while tying, carefully push back in with a flat-bladed knife. Rub generously with oil and salt.

2 Place on a rack in a baking dish. Bake the pork for 15 minutes, then reduce the heat to moderate 180°C (350°F/Gas 4). Bake for a further 1½–2 hours, or until the pork is cooked through. Cover and leave for 15 minutes before carving. Reserve any pan juices for gravy.

NUTRITION PER SERVE
Protein 57 g; Fat 6.5 g; Carbohydrate 7.5 g; Dietary Fibre 1 g; Cholesterol 120 mg; 1350 kJ (320 cal)

NOTE: If you prefer your rind really crackly, carefully remove it from the meat, cutting between the fat layer and the meat. Scrape off any excess fat and put the rind on a piece of aluminium foil. Place under a moderate grill, and grill until the rind has crackled.

If your butcher has not scored the pork rind, you must do this before cooking.

Spread the apple and prune stuffing over the meat side of the loin.

CHAMPAGNE APPLE SAUCE

Boil ¾ cup (185 ml) Champagne or sparkling wine in a pan for 1 minute. Add 4 green apples, peeled, cored and chopped, and ½ teaspoon finely grated lemon rind. Cover and simmer until the apple is tender. Stir in 1 tablespoon finely chopped fresh thyme and leave to cool for 5 minutes. Purée in a food processor. Gradually add 45 g chopped butter, processing between additions. Season to taste and serve warm. *Makes 2 cups (500 ml)*

PRUNE AND COINTREAU SAUCE

Place 250 g pitted prunes, 1 cup (250 ml) white wine, ½ cup (125 ml) orange juice, ¼ cup (60 ml) water and 1 tablespoon Cointreau in a pan. Bring to the boil, then reduce the heat and simmer for 10 minutes. Remove from the heat and add ¼ cup (60 ml) orange juice, ¼ cup (60 ml) water and 1 tablespoon Cointreau, and cool slightly. Pass through a fine sieve into a clean pan. Heat before serving and add 20 g chilled and chopped butter, a little at a time, whisking to thicken slightly. *Makes 1¼ cups (315 ml)*

CALVADOS GRAVY

Drain off all but 2 tablespoons of the pan juices from the baking dish. Place on the stove over moderate heat, add 1 tablespoon Calvados and stir. Cook for 1 minute. Remove from the heat, stir in 2 tablespoons plain flour and mix well. Return to the heat and cook for 2 minutes, stirring. Gradually add 1½ cups (375 ml) chicken stock and ½ cup (125 ml) unsweetened apple juice, and cook, stirring, until the gravy thickens. Season to taste. *Makes 2 cups (500 ml)*

Roll up the pork loin, securing with string or skewers at regular intervals.

Rub the pork loin with oil and salt before cooking to ensure a crisp rind.

STUFFINGS

The wonderful, fresh ingredients in stuffings add colour, flavour and texture to your roast. They also help turn everyday meals into special occasion feasts. All stuffings make enough to stuff a 4.5 kg turkey.

Citrus stuffing

Heat 1 tablespoon oil in a small pan. Add 2 finely chopped onions and cook until soft, then transfer to a large bowl and cool. Add 400 g sausage mince, 4 cups (320 g) fresh white breadcrumbs, 2 crushed garlic cloves, 1 tablespoon each grated lemon and orange rind, and 1 cup (120 g) finely chopped pecans and mix to combine. Season with salt and pepper and mix well. Suitable for roast turkey or pork.

Cashew and herb stuffing

Heat 60 g butter in a pan, add 1 chopped onion and 2 crushed garlic cloves and cook until golden. Transfer to a large bowl and allow to cool. Add 2½ cups (465 g) cooked brown rice, 1 cup (185 g) chopped dried apricots, ½ cup (80 g) chopped unsalted cashews, ¼ cup (15 g) chopped fresh parsley, 2 tablespoons chopped fresh mint, 1 tablespoon lemon juice and salt and pepper to taste. Suitable for roast turkey, pork or duck.

Rice and fruit stuffing

Place 3 cups (600 g) cooked long-grain rice, ½ cup (80 g) toasted pine nuts, 1½ cups (280 g) chopped dried apricots, 1½ cups (375 g) chopped pitted prunes, 4 sliced spring onions, 1 tablespoon finely grated orange rind, ⅓ cup (80 ml) orange juice, ½ teaspoon salt, a pinch of white pepper and 1 lightly beaten egg in a large bowl and mix to combine. Suitable for roast turkey, pork or duck.

Pistachio stuffing

Heat 2 tablespoons oil in a small pan and cook 5 finely chopped spring onions and 2 teaspoons grated fresh ginger for 2 minutes. Add 6 chopped bacon rashers and cook for 3–4 minutes. Transfer to a large bowl and allow to cool. Add 350 g pork and veal mince, 2 cups (160 g) fresh breadcrumbs, 1/3 cup (105 g) marmalade, 1/2 cup (30 g) chopped fresh parsley, 1 lightly beaten egg and 1 cup (150 g) pistachio kernels, season with salt and pepper and mix to combine. Suitable for roast turkey or pork.

Mushroom and tomato stuffing

Heat 2 tablespoons oil in a pan. Add 1 finely chopped onion, 3 crushed garlic cloves, 3 cups (270 g) finely sliced button mushrooms and 2 chopped tomatoes and cook for 5 minutes. Remove from the heat. Combine the mushroom mixture with 2 cups (370 g) cooked white or brown rice, 1/3 cup (50 g) finely chopped sundried tomatoes, 2 tablespoons shredded fresh basil, 1/3 cup (35 g) freshly grated Parmesan, 2 lightly beaten eggs, salt and pepper in a bowl and mix to combine. Suitable for roast turkey, pork or duck.

Ricotta and bacon stuffing

Finely chop 4 bacon rashers. Fry in a dry pan until crisp. Remove and set aside. In the same pan, heat 1 tablespoon oil and fry 2 chopped onions and 2 crushed garlic cloves until golden. Combine 2 cups (500 g) ricotta cheese, 1 lightly beaten egg, 1/3 cup (35 g) freshly grated Parmesan, 2 cups (160 g) fresh breadcrumbs, 1/2 cup (30 g) chopped fresh parsley, 2 tablespoons chopped fresh chives, 2 tablespoons chopped fresh tarragon, a pinch of nutmeg and the onion and bacon in a large bowl and mix to combine. Suitable for roast turkey or pork.

BAKED SALMON

Baked salmon is a perfect light alternative to traditional roast turkey or ham. Add a creamy cucumber, a hollandaise or dill mayonnaise sauce.

Preparation time: 10 minutes
Total cooking time: 30 minutes +
    45 minutes standing
Serves 8

2 kg whole salmon, cleaned,
    gutted and scaled
2 spring onions, roughly
    chopped
3 sprigs fresh dill
1/2 lemon, thinly sliced
6 black peppercorns
1/4 cup (60 ml) dry white wine
3 bay leaves

1 Preheat the oven to moderate 180°C (350°F/Gas 4). Rinse the salmon under cold running water and pat dry inside and out with paper towels. Stuff the salmon cavity with the spring onion, dill, lemon and peppercorns.

2 Brush a large double-layered piece of foil with oil and lay the salmon on the foil. Sprinkle on the wine and arrange the bay leaves over the top. Fold the foil over and wrap up, covering the salmon tightly.

3 Place the salmon in a shallow baking dish in the oven and cook for 30 minutes. Turn the oven off and leave the salmon in the oven for 45 minutes with the door closed.

4 Undo the foil and carefully peel away the skin of the salmon on the top side. Carefully flip the salmon onto the serving plate and remove the skin from the other side. Pull out the fins and any visible bones. Serve at room temperature with lemon slices.

NUTRITION PER SERVE
Protein 45 g; Fat 30 g; Carbohydrate 0 g; Dietary Fibre 0 g; Cholesterol 175 mg; 1930 kJ (459 cal)

NOTE: Do not open or remove the foil during the cooking or standing time. If the salmon is too long for your baking tray, remove the head before baking.

Stuff the fish with spring onion, dill, lemon and peppercorns.

Arrange the bay leaves over the top of the fish before wrapping it in foil.

CUCUMBER SAUCE

Cut 4 large Lebanese cucumbers in half lengthways and scoop out the seeds. Chop into 5 mm cubes and mix with 2 tablespoons chopped capers, 2 tablespoons chopped pickled gherkins and 2 tablespoons snipped fresh chives. Whisk together ½ cup (125 ml) cream, 2 tablespoons whole-egg mayonnaise, 1 tablespoon white wine or tarragon vinegar and 2 teaspoons French mustard. Add to the cucumber mixture and mix to combine. Season. Cover and refrigerate for 30 minutes before serving. *Makes 2 cups (500 ml)*

HOLLANDAISE

Melt 175 g butter, skim any froth from the surface and cool. Mix 4 egg yolks with 2 tablespoons water and whisk for 30 seconds, or until the mixture is pale and foamy. Place over very low heat and whisk for about 2–3 minutes, or until thick and the whisk leaves a trail—do not let the pan get too hot or the eggs will scramble. Remove from the heat. Add the cooled butter, a little at a time, whisking well between each addition. Do not use the milky butter whey in the bottom of the pan. Stir in 1 tablespoon lemon juice or vinegar, season and serve immediately. *Makes 1 cup (250 ml)*

DILL MAYONNAISE

Mix ¾ cup (185 g) whole-egg mayonnaise, ¼ cup (60 g) plain yoghurt, ¼ teaspoon finely grated lemon rind, 1½ tablespoons chopped fresh dill, 1 teaspoon lemon juice and a pinch of caster sugar. Season. Refrigerate for 1 hour before serving. *Makes 1 cup (250 ml)*

Tightly wrap the fish in foil, making sure it is completely covered.

Unwrap the fish, then peel away the skin on both sides before serving.

MUSHROOM NUT ROAST

Vegetarians need no longer miss out on a Christmas roast! Accompany this delicious roast with tomato, apricot or roasted pumpkin sauce.

Preparation time: 30 minutes
Total cooking time: 50 minutes
Serves 4–6

2 tablespoons olive oil
1 large onion, diced
2 cloves garlic, crushed
300 g cap mushrooms,
    finely chopped
1¹/₂ cups (235 g) brazil nuts
1¹/₃ cups (200 g) raw cashews
1 cup (125 g) grated Cheddar
¹/₄ cup (25 g) freshly grated
    Parmesan
1 egg, lightly beaten
2 tablespoons chopped fresh chives
1 cup (80 g) fresh wholemeal
    breadcrumbs

1 Preheat the oven to moderate 180°C (350°F/Gas 4). Grease an 11 x 21 cm loaf tin and line the base with baking paper. Heat the oil in a frying pan and add the onion, garlic and mushrooms. Cook over medium heat for 5 minutes, or until soft. Transfer to a large bowl and cool.

2 Place the brazil nuts on a baking tray in the oven for 2–3 minutes. Remove the tray from the oven, add the cashews to the brazil nuts and return to the oven for 3–5 minutes, or until the nuts are toasted but not burnt. Allow to cool slightly. Process the nuts in a food processor until finely chopped, but be careful not to overprocess.

3 Combine the nuts, mushroom mixture, cheeses, egg, chives and breadcrumbs. Mix well. Press firmly into the loaf tin and bake for 45 minutes, or until firm. Leave for 5 minutes, then turn out. Cut into slices and serve warm with tomato, roasted pumpkin or apricot sauce.

NUTRITION PER SERVE (6)
Protein 22 g; Fat 55 g; Carbohydrate 17 g; Dietary Fibre 7 g; Cholesterol 55 mg; 2725 kJ (650 cal)

Using a sharp knife, finely chop the cap mushrooms into small cubes.

Fry the onion, garlic and mushrooms in oil until they are soft.

Process the brazil nuts and cashews in a food processor until finely chopped.

Combine the ingredients well and press firmly into the prepared tin.

TOMATO SAUCE

Heat 30 ml olive oil in a pan and add 1 finely chopped onion and 1 crushed garlic clove. Fry for 5 minutes, or until the onion is soft, but not brown. Add a 400 g can chopped tomatoes, 1 teaspoon caster sugar, 1 tablespoon tomato paste and
⅓ cup (80 ml) water. Boil for 3–5 minutes, or until slightly thickened. Season to taste.
Makes 2 cups (500 ml)

ROASTED PUMPKIN SAUCE

Preheat the oven to moderately hot 200°C (400°F/ Gas 6). Cut 500 g unpeeled pumpkin into wedges and place in a baking dish. Combine 2 tablespoons olive oil with 2 crushed garlic cloves and drizzle over the
pumpkin. Season. Cook for 1 hour, or until the pumpkin is tender. Cool slightly. Dry-fry 2 teaspoons cumin seeds and 2 teaspoons coriander seeds for 5 minutes. Grind in a food processor or mortar and pestle. Remove the skin from the pumpkin and put the flesh, ground spices and 1 cup (250 ml) vegetable stock in a food processor. Purée until smooth, then transfer to a pan and heat through gently.
Makes 2 cups (500 ml)

APRICOT SAUCE

Place 250 g dried apricots in a pan with 1 cinnamon stick and 1 cardamom pod and enough cold water to cover. Bring to the boil, then reduce the heat and simmer for 15 minutes, or until the apricots are very soft. Cool, remove the spices and purée until smooth, adding
more water if needed. Cool completely and then stir in ⅓ cup (80 g) thick plain yoghurt.
Makes 2 cups (500 ml)

VEGETABLES

There are numerous delicious vegetable accompaniments to any of our roasts. Choose two or three of your favourites at their fresh, seasonal best to enhance and supplement your roast.

Celeriac and tarragon purée

Bring 2 cups (500 ml) vegetable stock, 2 cups (500 ml) water and the juice of 1 lemon to the boil. Add 3 peeled and chopped medium celeriacs, and cook for 10–15 minutes, or until tender. Drain and place in a food processor with 40 g butter and 1 tablespoon cream. Season and process until smooth. Add 1 tablespoon finely chopped fresh tarragon and process for a further 10 seconds. If it is too thick, add a little more cream. *Serves 6*

Vichy carrots

Trim and peel 1 kg carrots and cut into batons. Bring a pan of water to the boil and cook the carrots for 3–5 minutes, or until tender. Drain well. Melt 40 g butter in the pan and add 2 teaspoons of sugar. Return the carrots to the pan and toss together until the carrots start to colour a little. Add 2 teaspoons lemon juice and 2 teaspoons chopped fresh parsley and toss together. *Serves 6*

Broccoli with almonds

Cut 500 g broccoli into small florets. Heat 2 teaspoons oil and 20 g butter in a large frying pan, add 1 crushed garlic clove and 20 g flaked almonds. Cook for 1–2 minutes, or until the almonds are golden. Remove and set aside. Add the broccoli to the pan and toss, cooking for 3–5 minutes, or until the broccoli is just tender. Return the almonds to the pan and stir to combine. Serve hot. *Serves 4–6*

Honey-roasted pumpkin

Preheat the oven to moderately hot 200°C (400°F/Gas 6). Bring a large pan of water to the boil. Add 1 kg peeled butternut pumpkin, cut into 3 cm chunks, and 2 tablespoons honey. Boil for 3–5 minutes, or until just tender. Drain well. Place into a baking dish and drizzle with 1 tablespoon oil and 1 tablespoon honey. Toss to coat. Bake for 30–40 minutes, or until cooked through. Serve sprinkled with 2 teaspoons toasted sesame seeds. *Serves 6–8*

Left to right: Celeriac and tarragon purée; Vichy carrots; Broccoli with almonds; Honey-roasted pumpkin; Duchess potatoes; Brussels sprouts and chestnuts.

Duchess potatoes

Preheat the oven to moderate 180°C (350°F/Gas 4). Quarter 1 kg floury potatoes and steam or boil until just tender. Drain well, return to the pan and mash. Beat together 2 eggs, 1/3 cup (80 ml) cream and 1/4 teaspoon grated nutmeg. Season to taste with salt and black pepper. Add to the potato and mash until smooth and thick, but not too stiff. Allow to cool slightly. Put the potato in a piping bag with a 1.5 cm star nozzle. Pipe in swirls, not too close together, onto two greased baking trays. Brush with an egg yolk. Bake for 15–20 minutes, or until golden. *Serves 6–8*

Brussels sprouts and chestnuts

Make slits in the skins of 500 g chestnuts and put them in a pan. Cover with cold water and place over high heat. Bring to the boil, then reduce the heat and simmer for 10 minutes, drain and leave until cool enough to handle. Peel off the skins. Trim 1 kg sprouts and cut a cross in the bottom of each sprout. Bring a pan of water to the boil, add the sprouts and cook at a fast simmer for 5–8 minutes, or until just tender. Melt 30 g butter in a large frying pan and add the chestnuts. Cook until they begin to brown and then add the sprouts, tossing together. Season well with salt, pepper and nutmeg. *Serves 6–8*

Risotto-stuffed onions

Preheat the oven to moderately hot 200°C (400°F/Gas 6). Peel 8 medium onions (about 200 g each) and trim the bases, leaving them intact. Cut the top off the onions, leaving a wide opening. Place in a baking dish, drizzle with 1 tablespoon oil and bake for 1–1½ hours, or until golden. Heat 20 g butter in a pan, add 70 g chopped mushrooms and 20 g chopped prosciutto, and cook until the mushrooms have softened. Add ½ cup (110 g) arborio rice and stir until well coated in the butter. Gradually stir in 2½ cups (600 ml) hot chicken stock, about ½ cup at a time, making sure the liquid has been absorbed before adding another portion. When all the stock has been added, stir through 2 tablespoons grated Parmesan and 2 tablespoons chopped fresh parsley. Scoop out the flesh from the middle of each onion, leaving at least 3 layers of skin. Chop the remaining flesh and stir through the risotto mixture. Spoon the filling into the onion shells, piling a little on top. Return to the oven for a further 10 minutes and serve. *Serves 8*

Roasted parsnips

Preheat the oven to moderately hot 200°C (400°F/Gas 6). Peel 1 kg parsnips and cut in half lengthways. Boil in salted water for 5 minutes, then drain well. Put 2 tablespoons oil in a baking dish and put the dish in the oven to heat up. When the oil is hot, add the parsnip and toss in the oil. Season with salt and pepper and roast for about 30 minutes, or until well browned and crisp. Garnish with thick curls of Parmesan and sea salt. *Serves 6*

Braised fennel

Slice 4 small fennel bulbs into quarters. Reserve fronds. Melt 20 g butter in a frying pan and add 1 tablespoon sugar, stirring, then add the fennel, and cook until browned all over. Pour on 100 ml white wine and 150 ml chicken stock and bring to the boil, then reduce the heat and simmer, covered, for 10 minutes, or until tender. Remove the lid and turn up the heat until most of the liquid has evaporated and the sauce has become sticky. Stir in 1 tablespoon sour cream. Garnish with the reserved fronds.
Serves 8

Roast potatoes

Preheat the oven to moderate 180°C (350°F/Gas 4). Cut 1.2 kg all-purpose potatoes in half. Place in a pan of water and bring to the boil, then reduce the heat and simmer for about 5 minutes. Drain well and cool on paper towels. Scrape the rounded side of each potato with a fork to form a rough surface and place in a single layer on a greased baking tray. Melt 20 g butter, mix with 1 tablespoon oil, and brush half over the potatoes. Roast the potatoes for about 50 minutes, or until crisp and golden brown, brushing halfway through with the remaining butter and oil mixture. *Serves 6–8*

Leeks in a white sauce

Trim and wash 2 leeks, cut in half lengthways and then into 5 cm pieces. Heat 30 g butter in a heavy-based pan, add the leeks and cook for 5 minutes, turning gently, or until tender. Place in an ovenproof serving dish. Melt 20 g butter in a pan, add 1 tablespoon plain flour and stir over medium heat for 1 minute. Remove from the heat and gradually add 1 cup (250 ml) milk. Return to the heat, stirring until the sauce boils and thickens. Pour over the top of the leeks. Sprinkle over 2 tablespoons grated cheese and 1 tablespoon dry breadcrumbs. Place under a hot grill for 2–3 minutes, or until crisp and golden on top. *Serves 4–6*

Left to right: Risotto-stuffed onions; Roasted parsnips; Braised fennel; Roast potatoes; Leeks in a white sauce.

MIXED SEAFOOD SALAD

Preparation time: 1 hour +
    1 hour refrigeration
Total cooking time: 12 minutes
Serves 8

24 cooked king prawns
16 cooked yabbies
½ cup (125 ml) white wine
pinch of dried thyme
pinch of dried tarragon or
    a bay leaf
24 scallops, with roe attached
400 g skinless salmon or trout
6 hard-boiled eggs
150 g mesclun
    (mixed lettuce leaves)
2 tablespoons coarsely chopped
    fresh flat-leaf parsley
2 avocados, sliced
2 tablespoons lemon juice

DILL VINAIGRETTE
½ cup (125 ml) extra virgin
    olive oil
2 tablespoons white wine
    vinegar
1 teaspoon sugar
2 teaspoons Dijon mustard
1 tablespoon chopped
    fresh dill

GREEN GODDESS DRESSING
2 egg yolks
2 teaspoons Dijon mustard
3 tablespoons lemon juice
1 cup (250 ml) olive oil
4 anchovy fillets, chopped
1 clove garlic, crushed
¼ cup (60 g) sour cream
¼ cup (15 g) chopped fresh
    mixed herbs

1 Peel and devein the prawns. Place the yabbies on their backs, exposing the underside. Cut through below the base of the head to remove and discard the head piece. Using scissors, cut down either side of the soft undershell, pull back and remove the flesh in one piece.

2 Put 1 cup (250 ml) water in a pan and add the wine, herbs and a pinch of salt and pepper. Bring to the boil, then reduce the heat and simmer for 5 minutes. Add the scallops and poach for 1–2 minutes, or until they have just turned white, then remove with a slotted spoon and drain on a wire rack. Add the fish fillets and poach until cooked and just tender, remove with a slotted spoon and drain on a wire rack. Break into large pieces.

3 To make the dill vinaigrette, combine all the ingredients and whisk until blended, then season.

4 Combine the prawns, yabbies, scallops and fish in a bowl. Pour the dill vinaigrette into the bowl, cover and refrigerate for 1 hour. Peel and slice the eggs, reserving 2 yolks.

5 To make the green goddess dressing, process the egg yolks, Dijon mustard and 2 tablespoons lemon juice in a food processor or blender for 30 seconds, or until light and creamy. With the motor running, add the oil in a thin, steady stream, increasing the flow as the mayonnaise thickens. Add 2–4 teaspoons lemon juice, the anchovy fillets, garlic, sour cream and fresh herbs. Season with salt and freshly ground white pepper and pulse for 30 seconds to combine the mixture well.

6 Place half the lettuce leaves in the base of a deep serving bowl. Arrange about half the seafood on the lettuce, reserving the dill

vinaigrette. Sprinkle with half the parsley, top with half the avocado, drizzle with half the lemon juice, then finish with half the sliced eggs,

Peel the prawns and then remove the intestinal tract running down the back.

Discard the head piece of the yabbies and try to remove the flesh in one piece.

Poach the scallops in a mixture of wine and herbs.

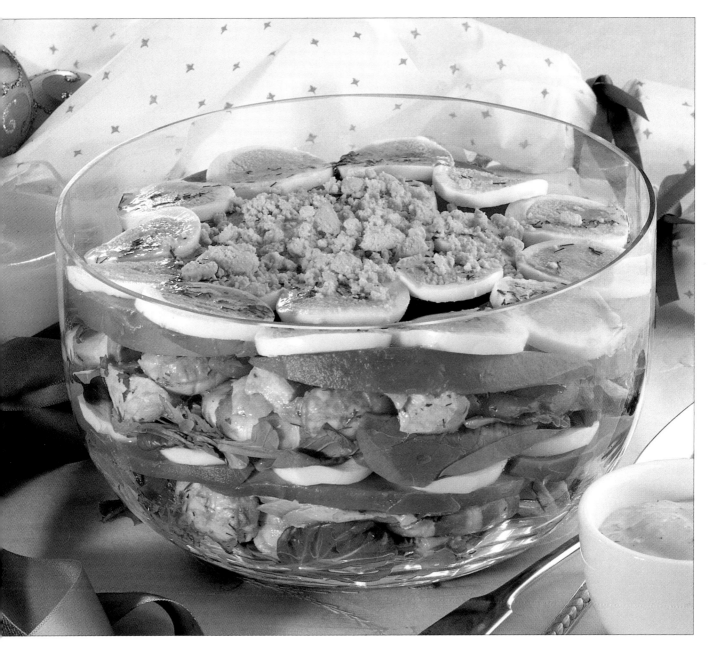

including the extra whites. Season with salt and freshly ground black pepper. Repeat the layers and season to taste with salt and freshly ground black pepper again. Drizzle with the reserved dill vinaigrette. Crumble the reserved egg yolks over the top and serve with green goddess dressing.

NUTRITION PER SERVE
Protein 30 g; Fat 63 g; Carbohydrate 1.6 g; Dietary Fibre 1 g; Cholesterol 337 mg; 2936 kJ (700 cal)

Drain the poached fish fillets on a wire rack and break into large pieces.

Whisk together all the ingredients for the vinaigrette and season well.

Process the green goddess dressing for 30 seconds to achieve the right consistency.

POTATO SALAD

Preparation time: 15 minutes
Total cooking time: 25 minutes
Serves 8

8 large waxy potatoes,
　　chopped into 2 cm cubes
1/3 cup (90 g) whole-egg
　　mayonnaise
1 1/2 cups (45 g) fresh
　　coriander leaves
2 tablespoons olive oil
1 teaspoon lemon juice
1 teaspoon olive oil
6 small spring onions,
　　very thinly sliced
1 tablespoon balsamic
　　vinegar
4 tomatoes, seeded and
　　finely chopped
300 g bacon, thinly sliced
1 hard-boiled egg
1 1/2 cups (45 g) snow pea
　　sprouts or watercress

1 Boil or microwave the potato until just tender—do not overcook. Refresh under cold water, drain and place in a large bowl.

2 Put the whole-egg mayonnaise, coriander leaves, olive oil and lemon juice in a blender and process until smooth. Season to taste with salt and ground black pepper.

3 Heat the oil in a frying pan, add the spring onion and balsamic vinegar and stir. Cook over low heat for 3 minutes, cool, and then add to the mayonnaise mixture with the chopped tomato. Pour over the potato and toss to coat. Cover with plastic wrap and refrigerate until ready to serve.

4 Fry the bacon until very crispy and drain on paper towels. Grate or finely chop the hard-boiled egg. Add the bacon, egg and snow pea sprouts to the salad, toss and serve.

NUTRITION PER SERVE
Protein 11 g; Fat 11 g; Carbohydrate
20 g; Dietary Fibre 3.5 g; Cholesterol
40 mg; 935 kJ (225 cal)

Add the mayonnaise and tomato mixture to the potato and toss to coat.

Fry the bacon until crispy and drain well on paper towels.

ORANGE POPPY SEED VEGETABLES

Preparation time: 20 minutes
Total cooking time: 1 hour
Serves 6–8

500 g new potatoes, halved
6 parsnips, peeled and quartered
    lengthways
500 g orange sweet potato, diced
350 g baby carrots, peeled, with tops
    left on
6 pickling onions, halved
1/3 cup (80 ml) oil
2 tablespoons poppy seeds
200 g triple cream brie,
    thinly sliced

ORANGE DRESSING
1/2 cup (125 ml) orange juice
2 cloves garlic, crushed
1 tablespoon Dijon mustard
1 teaspoon white wine vinegar
1 teaspoon sesame oil

1 Preheat the oven to moderately hot 200°C (400°F/Gas 6). Place the potato, parsnip, sweet potato, carrots, onion and oil in a large, deep baking dish. Toss to coat all the vegetables with the oil. Bake the vegetables for 50–60 minutes, or until they are crisp and tender, tossing every 15 minutes. Sprinkle with the poppy seeds.

2 To make the orange dressing, whisk the orange juice, garlic, Dijon mustard, vinegar and sesame oil together in a bowl.

3 Pour the dressing over the warm vegetables and toss to coat well. Transfer the vegetables to a large bowl, top with the brie and serve immediately, while still warm.

NUTRITION PER SERVE (8)
Protein 10 g; Fat 17 g; Carbohydrate 32 g; Dietary Fibre 6.5 g; Cholesterol 25 mg; 1360 kJ (325 cal)

Bake the vegetables until they are crisp and tender, then sprinkle with poppy seeds.

Whisk the orange dressing ingredients together in a bowl.

VEGETABLE TART WITH SALSA VERDE

Preparation time: 30 minutes +
30 minutes refrigeration
Total cooking time: 50 minutes
Serves 6

PASTRY
1³/4 cups (220 g) plain flour
120 g butter, chilled and cubed
1/4 cup (60 ml) cream
1–2 tablespoons iced water

SALSA VERDE
1 clove garlic
2 cups (40 g) firmly packed fresh
    flat-leaf parsley
1/3 cup (80 ml) extra virgin
    olive oil
1/4 cup (15 g) chopped fresh dill
1¹/2 tablespoons Dijon mustard
1 tablespoon red wine vinegar
1 tablespoon baby capers,
    drained

FILLING
1 large (250 g) Desiree potato,
    chopped into 2 cm cubes
1 tablespoon olive oil
2 cloves garlic, crushed
1 red capsicum, chopped into
    3 cm squares
1 red onion, sliced into rings
2 zucchini, sliced
2 tablespoons chopped fresh dill
1 tablespoon chopped fresh thyme
1 tablespoon baby capers, drained
150 g marinated artichoke
    hearts, drained
²/3 cup (30 g) baby English spinach
    leaves

1 Sift the flour and ¹/2 teaspoon salt into a large bowl and rub in the butter with your fingers until the mixture resembles fine breadcrumbs. Add the cream and water and mix with a flat-bladed knife until the mixture just comes together in small beads. Gently gather the dough into a ball and turn out onto a lightly floured work surface. Flatten into a disc, cover with plastic wrap, and refrigerate for 30 minutes.

2 Preheat the oven to moderately hot 200°C (400°F/Gas 6). Lightly grease a 27 cm shallow fluted flan tin with a removable base.

3 Roll the dough out between 2 sheets of baking paper until large enough to line the flan tin. Remove the paper and carefully lift the pastry into the flan tin, pressing it gently into the fluted sides. Trim any excess pastry. Line the pastry with crumpled baking paper and fill with baking beads or rice. Place the flan tin on a baking tray and bake for 15–20 minutes. Remove the paper and beads, reduce the oven to moderate 180°C (350°F/Gas 4) and bake for a further 20 minutes, or until the pastry case is dry and golden.

4 Meanwhile, to make the salsa verde, combine all the ingredients in a food processor and blend until almost smooth.

5 To make the filling, boil, steam or microwave the potato until just tender, but do not overcook. Drain and set aside.

6 Heat the oil in a large frying pan and add the garlic, capsicum and onion. Cook over medium–high heat for 3 minutes, stirring often. Add the zucchini, dill, thyme and capers and cook for 3 minutes more, stirring frequently. Add the potato and artichokes, reduce the heat to

low and cook for 3–4 minutes, or until the potato and artichokes are heated through. Season to taste with salt and freshly ground black pepper.

Rub the butter into the flour and salt with your fingers.

Use a flat-bladed knife to combine the mixture until it comes together in beads.

Press the pastry gently into the sides of the greased flan tin.

7 To assemble the tart, spread ¼ cup of the salsa verde over the base of the pastry case. Spoon the vegetable mixture into the case and drizzle with half the remaining salsa verde. Pile the spinach in the centre and drizzle with remaining salsa verde. Serve immediately.

NUTRITION PER SERVE
Protein 5.5 g; Fat 30 g; Carbohydrate 27 g; Dietary Fibre 3.5 g; Cholesterol 50 mg; 1590 kJ (380 cal)

Bake the pastry case for 20 minutes, or until it is dry and golden.

Process the salsa verde ingredients until the mix is almost smooth.

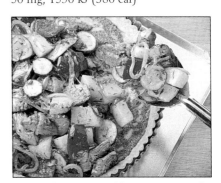

Spoon the hot vegetable mixture into the pastry case.

PICKLED PRAWNS

Preparation time: 20 minutes +
    48 hours refrigeration
Total cooking time: nil
Serves 4–6

40 large cooked prawns
1 fennel bulb, or 2 baby fennel bulbs
   (600 g)
2 small red onions, thinly sliced
rind of 2 oranges, cut into
   thin strips
rind of 2 limes, cut into
   thin strips
6–8 tablespoons lime juice
   (juice of 4 limes)
1/3 cup (80 ml) orange juice
1 cup (250 ml) olive oil
1/2 cup (125 ml) tarragon
   vinegar
2 red birdseye chillies, finely
   sliced
1 teaspoon sugar

1 Peel and devein the prawns, leaving the tails intact. Slice the fennel thinly, removing any tough outer leaves first and reserving some of the green fronds for use as a garnish. Place the prawns, fennel, onion and orange and lime rind in a non-metallic container and mix well.

2 Mix the lime juice, orange juice, olive oil, tarragon vinegar, chilli, sugar and 1 teaspoon salt together and pour over the prawn mixture. Cover, either with a lid or plastic wrap, and refrigerate for 48 hours. Stir the mixture once or twice during this time to make sure every part of the prawn comes into contact with the marinade.

3 Garnish the prawns with the reserved fennel fronds and serve with crusty bread and a mixed salad.

NUTRITION PER SERVE (6)
Protein 6.5 g; Fat 20 g; Carbohydrate 7 g; Dietary Fibre 3.5 g; Cholesterol 35 mg; 1731 kJ (414 cal)

Thinly slice the fennel, reserving some of the fronds for garnish.

Stir the mixture during the marinating time to ensure the prawns are evenly covered.

CHICKEN BALLOTTINE

Preparation time: 45 minutes
Total cooking time: 1 hour
20 minutes + standing
Serves 8

1 x 1.8 kg chicken, boned
(ask your butcher to do this)
190 g chicken breast fillet
1 tablespoon olive oil

FILLING
1/3 cup (60 g) chopped dried
apricots
1/3 cup (60 g) chopped
dried figs
1 cup (80 g) fresh white
breadcrumbs
190 g chicken mince
60 g sliced prosciutto, chopped
1 tablespoon chopped glacé ginger
1 tablespoon chopped fresh chives
1 egg, lightly beaten
2 tablespoons chopped fresh
parsley

1 Preheat the oven to moderate 180°C (350°F/Gas 4). Turn the wing and drumstick flesh inside the chicken and lay the chicken out flat, skin-side-down.

2 Place the fillet in a plastic bag and, using your hand, flatten out to an even thickness. Cover the chicken and fillet and refrigerate.

3 To make the filling, place the apricots and the figs in a small bowl, cover with boiling water and leave for 3 minutes to soften, then drain. Combine with the remaining filling ingredients and season.

4 Place the filling over the chicken and top with the fillet. Roll the chicken to enclose the filling, tucking the ends in as you go. Use a sewing needle and double cotton to sew up the chicken and secure the filling. Tie the chicken with string to help retain its shape. Brush with oil and place in a baking dish. Bake for 1 hour 20 minutes, or until golden brown and cooked through. Cover with foil and leave to stand for 10–15 minutes before removing the string and thread. Cut into slices to serve.

NUTRITION PER SERVE
Protein 60 g; Fat 15 g; Carbohydrate 14 g; Dietary Fibre 2 g; Cholesterol 210 mg; 1785 kJ (427 cal)

Place the filling over the boned chicken, cover with the fillet and roll up.

Tie the chicken securely with string to ensure it keeps its shape while cooking.

RAISED PORK PIE

Preparation time: 20 minutes +
    refrigeration + overnight setting
Total cooking time: 65 minutes
Serves 6

1.2 kg minced pork
2/3 cup (90 g) pistachio nuts,
    shelled and chopped
2 green apples, peeled and finely
    chopped
6 fresh sage leaves, finely chopped
4 cups (500 g) plain flour
150 g butter
2 eggs, lightly beaten
1 egg yolk
200 ml vegetable stock
200 ml unsweetened apple juice
2 teaspoons gelatine

1 Preheat the oven to moderately hot 200°C (400°F/Gas 6). Put the pork, pistachio nuts, apple and sage leaves in a bowl, mix well and season. Fry a piece of the mixture to taste and adjust the seasoning. Cover and refrigerate. Wrap a piece of plastic wrap around a 6 cm high, 20 cm straight-sided tin, then turn the tin over, and grease the outside base and side of the tin.

2 Put the flour and 1 teaspoon salt in a bowl and make a well in the centre. Put the butter in a pan with 210 ml water, bring to the boil and add to the flour, with the eggs. Mix with a wooden spoon until combined, then turn out onto a work surface and bring the mixture together to form a smooth dough. Wrap in plastic wrap and refrigerate for 10 minutes.

3 Cut off a third of the pastry and wrap in plastic wrap—do not refrigerate. Roll the remainder into a circle large enough to just cover the

Combine the ingredients for the filling and season to taste.

The dough must be combined to a smooth consistency.

Cover the outside of the tin with the pastry, working fast so that it does not set.

outside of the tin. Lift onto a rolling pin and place over the tin, working fast before the pastry sets. Refrigerate until the pastry hardens. Carefully pull out the tin and remove the plastic wrap. Attach a paper collar made of 2 layers of greased baking paper around the outside of the pastry so it fits snugly and secure with a paper clip at the top and bottom. Fill the pie, then roll out the remaining pastry to form a lid. Attach it to the base with some water, pressing or crimping it to make it look neat. Cut a small hole in the top of the pie.

4 Put the pie on a baking tray, bake for 40 minutes and check the pastry top. If it is still pale, bake for another 10 minutes, then remove the paper. Brush with egg yolk mixed with 1 tablespoon water and bake for another 15 minutes, or until the sides are brown. Cool completely.

5 Bring the stock and half the apple juice to the boil. Sprinkle the gelatine over the surface of the remaining apple juice in a jug and leave to go spongy, then pour into the stock and mix until the gelatine dissolves. Place a small funnel (piping nozzles work well) in the hole of the pie and pour in a little of the gelatine mixture, leave to settle and then pour in some more until the pie is full. Fill the pie completely so there are no gaps when the gelatine mixture sets. Leave to set overnight.

NUTRITION PER SERVE
Protein 60 g; Fat 35 g; Carbohydrate 72 g; Dietary Fibre 5.5 g; Cholesterol 257 mg; 3545 kJ (845 cal)

NOTE: If wrapped tightly with plastic wrap, pork pies will last in the refrigerator for up to 4–5 days.

The greased paper collar should fit snugly around the outside of the pastry.

Cut a small hole in the top of the pie to allow the gelatine to be poured in.

Gradually pour the gelatine into the cooked and cooled pie until it is full.

TURKEY LEFTOVERS

Roast turkey is a seasonal dish for most people—Christmas and, for some, Thanksgiving. If the thought of days of turkey sandwiches is all a bit overwhelming, here are some tasty alternatives.

Turkey empanadas

Heat 1 tablespoon oil in a frying pan, add 1 small finely chopped onion and 1 crushed garlic clove. Cook over medium heat for 2 minutes, then add 2 teaspoons paprika, 1 teaspoon ground cumin and ½ teaspoon ground cinnamon, and stir until fragrant. Add 2 tablespoons sherry, 400 g can puréed tomatoes and 400 g finely chopped turkey. Simmer for about 10 minutes, or until thick. Remove from the heat, stir in ½ cup (110 g) chopped pitted green olives, 3 chopped hard-boiled eggs and 1 tablespoon chopped fresh parsley, and season. Transfer to a bowl and allow to cool. Using 4½ sheets of ready-rolled shortcrust pastry, cut 12 cm rounds from each sheet (you will need 18 rounds). Place 1½ tablespoons of the mixture on one half of each round, brush the edge lightly with water and fold the pastry over to enclose the filling. Press the edges with a fork to seal. Deep-fry the empanadas in batches for about 3–5 minutes, or until golden brown. Drain on paper towels.
Makes 18

Leek, turkey and sweet corn soup

Heat 20 g butter in a large pan and add 1 thinly sliced leek. Cook over medium heat until soft. Add 3½ cups (875 ml) chicken stock and 420 g can creamed corn. Season with salt and pepper. Bring to the boil and then reduce the heat and simmer for 5 minutes. Add 250 g shredded cooked turkey.
Serves 4

Left to right: Turkey empanadas; Leek, turkey and sweet corn soup; Potato and apple salad; Turkey filo parcels; Turkey san choy bau.

Potato and apple salad

Cut 4 spring onions into thin strips and fry until crisp. Boil 750 g new potatoes until just tender; drain and allow to cool, then cut in half. Cut an unpeeled red apple into thin wedges and toss with 1 tablespoon lemon juice. Boil 2 thickly sliced zucchini until tender, then drain and refresh in cold water. For the dressing, combine 1/2 cup (125 g) whole-egg mayonnaise, 3 teaspoons Dijon mustard, 1 tablespoon wholegrain mustard and 2 tablespoons lemon juice. Season to taste. Cut 400 g turkey meat into thin strips and toss with the potato, apple, zucchini, 2 tablespoons chopped fresh parsley and the dressing until combined. Top with the crispy spring onion.

Serves 6

Turkey filo parcels

Preheat the oven to moderate 180°C (350°F/Gas 4). Heat 20 g butter in a large pan, add 200 g sliced mushrooms and 4 diced rashers bacon. Cook over high heat until the mushrooms are soft and there is no liquid left. Stir through 350 g chopped, cooked turkey, 150 g ricotta, 2 sliced spring onions and 1/4 cup (15 g) shredded fresh basil. Season with black pepper. Cover 24 sheets of filo pastry with a damp tea towel. Working with 3 sheets at a time, brush each layer with melted butter. Cut the pastry into 3 strips. Place 1 tablespoon of filling at the end of each strip and fold the pastry over to form a triangle. Continue folding until you reach the end of the pastry. Repeat with the remaining pastry and filling. Place on a baking tray, brush with butter and sprinkle with sesame seeds. Bake in the oven for 35 minutes, or until crisp.

Makes 24

Turkey san choy bau

Soak 8 small iceberg lettuce leaves in cold water while preparing the filling. Soak 5 dried Chinese mushrooms in a bowl of boiling water for 15 minutes, or until soft. Drain, discard stems and finely chop. Heat 1 teaspoon sesame oil and 2 teaspoons oil in a pan, add 2 crushed cloves garlic, 1 tablespoon grated fresh ginger and 100 g thinly sliced canned baby corn, and toss over heat until fragrant. Add 300 g finely chopped cooked turkey, the Chinese mushrooms, 1/2 cup (90 g) finely chopped water chestnuts, 100 g bean sprouts, 2 chopped spring onions, 1 tablespoon chopped fresh coriander, 1 teaspoon sugar, 1 tablespoon oyster sauce and 1 tablespoon soy sauce. Toss the mixture well to heat. Drain the lettuce and carefully pat dry. Spoon the turkey filling into each lettuce cup and serve.

Serves 4

HAM LEFTOVERS

A 7 kg ham serves around 20 people. But don't worry, leftover ham can be kept wrapped in a damp tea towel in the refrigerator for up to 10 days. Try some of these delicious ways of finishing it off.

Ham and cider casserole

Preheat the oven to moderately hot 200°C (400°F/Gas 6). Heat 1 tablespoon butter in a heavy-based pan and add 1 chopped onion. Fry for 2–3 minutes, or until tender, then add 2 sliced leeks and continue frying until the leeks are cooked through. Stir in 2 crushed garlic cloves. Place the onion and leek mixture in the base of an ovenproof dish. Scatter with 400 g (8 slices) chopped ham, season with pepper and pour on 100 ml apple cider. Spoon 1 can (300 g) rinsed, drained butter beans over and around the ham and sprinkle with ⅓ cup (25 g) fresh breadcrumbs and 1 tablespoon freshly grated Parmesan. Dot with 20 g butter and bake for 20 minutes. *Serves 4*

Layered cob

Place 2 red capsicums under a hot grill, turning occasionally, until the skin blackens and blisters. Cool under a tea towel or in a plastic bag, then peel away the skin and cut the flesh into slices. Slice 500 g eggplant and grill until golden on both sides. Briefly steam 400 g washed and trimmed English spinach until wilted, allow to cool, and squeeze out any excess liquid. Cut a large round from the top of a 22 cm cob loaf and reserve. Scoop out the white bread, leaving a 1 cm border. Brush the inside of the loaf and the inside of the lid with 2 tablespoons oil, combined with

2 crushed garlic cloves. Place half the eggplant slices in the bottom, layer the red capsicum on top, then 150 g sliced ham. Top with 2 cups (500 g) ricotta mixed with 2 tablespoons chopped fresh parsley, ¼ cup (25 g) grated Parmesan and season with salt and pepper. Spread the spinach leaves over the top, then add the remaining eggplant. Put the lid on and wrap tightly with plastic wrap. Place a plate on top and weigh down with some cans and leave overnight. *Serves 6–8*

Left to right: Ham and cider casserole; Layered cob; Split pea and ham soup; Ham and leek pie; Ham, bean and tomato salad.

Split pea and ham soup

Rinse 500 g yellow split peas in cold water, then drain. Place the peas, your leftover ham bone, 2 chopped carrots, 2 chopped celery sticks, 1 large chopped onion, 2 bay leaves and 3 litres water in a pan, cover and bring to the boil. Reduce the heat and simmer, partly covered, for 2 hours, or until the peas are tender. Skim off any scum that rises to the surface. Remove the ham bone and remove the meat from the bone, discarding any fat or skin. Finely chop the ham and set aside. Remove the bay leaves. Purée the soup until smooth, adding a little more water if needed, then stir in the ham. Season with pepper and salt if needed. Note: This soup thickens on standing and it's great to freeze too. *Serves 8*

Ham and leek pie

Preheat the oven to moderately hot 200°C (400°F/Gas 6). Boil 2 medium potatoes until just tender and then slice. Melt 20 g butter in a frying pan, add 2 sliced leeks and cook until golden. Add 300 g ham cut into large cubes and toss to combine. Place the potato slices in the bottom of a greased 23 cm pie plate, top with the ham and leek mixture. Pour in 1/3 cup (80 ml) cream, combined with 2 lightly beaten eggs and 2 tablespoons chopped fresh parsley. Sprinkle with 1/2 cup (60 g) grated cheese. Wet the edge of the pie plate with a little water, place 1 sheet thawed ready-rolled puff pastry on top, trim the edges and press down to seal. Cut two slits in the top of the pastry and decorate with any leftover pastry. Bake for 40 minutes, or until golden. *Serves 6–8*

Ham, bean and tomato salad

Top and tail 200 g green beans and 200 g sugar snap peas. Cut the beans on the diagonal into 4 cm lengths. Place the beans, peas and 200 g frozen broad beans in a pan of boiling water and cook for 1 minute. Drain and refresh in cold water. Discard the outer skin from the broad beans. Cut 200 g sliced ham into thin strips and combine with the beans and peas, 250 g halved cherry tomatoes, 3/4 cup (115 g) cashews, 2 tablespoons chopped fresh parsley and 2 tablespoons chopped fresh chives in a large bowl. For the dressing, combine 1/4 cup (60 ml) olive oil, 2 tablespoons cider vinegar, 1/2 teaspoon sugar and 2 tablespoons chopped fresh mint in a screw-top jar and shake well. Pour the dressing over the salad and toss well. Season. *Serves 6*

PUDDINGS AND DESSERTS

FEW THINGS sum up the Christmas season quite so well as a steaming, hot Christmas pudding. Add some brandy butter or vanilla custard and you have a dessert to look forward to all year. But given the festive spirit, there's no need to stop at just one. Why not try some trifle or berries in Champagne jelly as well? And what would Christmas be without mince pies and Christmas cake?

BOILED CHRISTMAS PUDDING

Preparation time: 40 minutes
+ 2 nights standing
Total cooking time: 7 hours
Serves 10–12

1²/₃ cups (310 g) mixed
   dried fruit
¼ cup (45 g) mixed peel
4 cups (500 g) mixed sultanas,
   currants and raisins
½ cup (125 ml) brown ale
2 tablespoons rum or brandy
rind and juice of 1 orange
rind and juice of 1 lemon
225 g suet, grated
1¹/₃ cups (245 g) soft brown
   sugar
3 eggs, lightly beaten
2¹/₂ cups (200 g) fresh white
   breadcrumbs
³/₄ cup (90 g) self-raising flour
1 teaspoon mixed spice
¼ teaspoon freshly grated nutmeg
²/₃ cup (100 g) blanched almonds,
   chopped

1 Finely chop the mixed dried fruit. Place in a large bowl with the mixed peel, sultanas, currants, raisins, ale, rum, orange and lemon rind and juice. Cover and leave overnight.

2 Mix the fruit mixture with the remaining ingredients and a pinch of salt in a large bowl. Leave to stand for 10 minutes to thicken.

3 Cut an 80 cm square from a clean piece of calico or an old tea towel and boil it for 20 minutes. Wring out (wearing rubber gloves to prevent scalding) and spread on a clean work surface. Dust the calico with a thick layer of plain flour, leaving a border around the edge. Spread the flour out with your hands—it is important that you get an even covering because the flour forms a seal to prevent the pudding absorbing any water. Place the pudding mixture onto the centre of the calico and bring the points of the material together. Gather in all the excess material, trying to make the folds neat and even (they will leave an imprint on the finished pudding). Tie the top tightly with a piece of unwaxed string—no water should get in. Tie a loop into the end of one of the pieces of string to act as a handle. Hook a wooden spoon handle through the loop and lower the pudding into a pan of boiling water. The pudding should not rest on the base of the pan. Make sure the pan is large enough for the pudding to move around.

4 Cover the pan and boil for 5 hours. If the water level drops, add more boiling water around the edge of the pudding. Remove from the water and hang in a well-ventilated, dry place where it will not touch anything. Make sure the calico ends all hang to one side so they do not drip all over the pudding. Leave overnight.

5 Untie the cloth and, if there are damp patches at the top, spread it out to make sure it dries. When it is dry, re-wrap and tie with a new piece of string. The pudding will store hanging in a cool, dry place for up to 4 months. To serve, boil for 2 hours, hang for 15 minutes, then remove from the cloth and cut into wedges.

NUTRITION PER SERVE (12)
Protein 7.5 g; Fat 20 g; Carbohydrate 76 g; Dietary Fibre 5.5 g; Cholesterol 60 mg; 2211 kJ (528 cal)

Mix all the ingredients together in a large bowl and leave for 10 minutes.

Dust a calico square with a thick layer of plain flour, spreading it with your hands.

Put the pudding mixture in the centre of the calico square and draw the material up.

When gathering all the material together, try to keep the folds as neat as possible.

Tie a loop in the string sealing the pudding and use this as a handle.

Using the string handle, lower the pudding into a large pan of boiling water.

STEAMED CHRISTMAS PUDDING

Preparation time: 40 minutes + overnight standing
Total cooking time: 8 hours
Serves 10–12

4 cups (500 g) mixed sultanas,
    currants and raisins
1²/₃ cups (310 g) mixed dried
    fruit, chopped
¼ cup (45 g) mixed peel
½ cup (125 ml) brown ale
2 tablespoons rum or brandy
juice and rind of 1 orange
juice and rind of 1 lemon
225 g suet, grated (see Note)
1¹/₃ cups (245 g) soft brown sugar
3 eggs, lightly beaten
2½ cups (200 g) fresh white
    breadcrumbs
¾ cup (90 g) self-raising flour
1 teaspoon mixed spice
¼ teaspoon freshly grated nutmeg
²/₃ cup (100 g) blanched almonds,
    roughly chopped

1 Place the sultanas, currants, raisins, dried fruit, mixed peel, ale, rum, orange and lemon juice and rind into a large bowl. Cover and leave overnight.

2 The next day, mix together the fruit mixture, suet, brown sugar, eggs, breadcrumbs, flour, spices, almonds and a pinch of salt in a large bowl. The mixture should fall from the spoon—if it is too stiff, add a little more ale. Place a 2 litre pudding basin on a trivet in a large pan with a lid, which will comfortably hold it, and pour in enough water to reach halfway up the side of the basin. Remove the basin and put the water on to boil.

3 Grease the pudding basin and line the base with a circle of baking paper. Fill with the pudding mixture. Cut a sheet of baking paper and a sheet of foil big enough to fit comfortably over the top of the basin and come halfway down the sides. Lay the baking paper on top of the foil, grease the paper, then make a pleat in the centre. Put the cover, paper-side-down on top of the pudding and fold everything down over the edge. Cover with a lid if your basin has one, or tie a double piece of string securely around the rim of the basin, just under the lip, and make a handle which runs across the top with another piece of string.

Place the basin carefully on the trivet in the pan and turn the water down to a fast simmer. Cover the pan and steam for 8 hours, replenishing with boiling water when necessary. If you want to keep your pudding and reheat it later, then steam it for 6 hours and steam it for another 2 hours on the day you would like to eat it. Store in a cool, dry place for up to 3 months.

NUTRITION PER SERVE (12)
Protein 7 g; Fat 20 g; Carbohydrate 75 g; Dietary Fibre 5 g; Cholesterol 60 mg; 2167 kJ (518 cal)

NOTE: Buy suet from your butcher.
    Metal pudding basins are better heat conductors than ceramic basins so puddings will cook more quickly in them. Check the pudding about 30 minutes before the cooking time is up. To test, insert a skewer into the centre of the pudding. If it comes out clean, the pudding is cooked.

Mix all the ingredients together, adding more ale if the mixture is too dry.

Cut a round of baking paper to fit the base of the pudding basin.

Grate the suet with the rough side of a cheese grater.

Make a pleat in the foil and paper cover so the pudding can expand when cooking.

Cover the pudding with the greased paper facing down.

Tie the cover securely to the basin with string and make a handle across the top.

SWEET SAUCES

Sinfully thick and creamy, these sauces make perfect accompaniments for Christmas cakes or puddings. For something a little lighter, try serving them with fresh fruit.

Left to right: Brandy butter; Brandy cream sauce; Zabaglione; Whisky sauce; Crème Anglaise; Vanilla custard.

Brandy butter

Using electric beaters, beat 250 g softened unsalted butter and 1½ cups (185 g) sifted icing sugar until smooth and creamy. Gradually add ¼ cup (60 ml) brandy, beating thoroughly. Refrigerate until required. *Makes about 1 cup (250 ml)*

Brandy cream sauce

Beat 2 egg yolks and ⅓ cup (90 g) caster sugar until thick and pale and all the sugar has dissolved. Stir in ⅓ cup (80 ml) brandy and fold in 1 cup (250 ml) cream. Beat 2 egg whites in a clean, dry bowl until soft peaks form. Fold into the sauce and serve immediately. *Makes 1½ cups (375 ml)*

Zabaglione

In a heatproof bowl, beat together 8 egg yolks and ⅓ cup (90 g) caster sugar with electric beaters until thick and pale. Put the bowl over a simmering pan of water and beat continuously, gradually adding 1¼ cups (315 ml) Marsala. Beat for 5 minutes, or until thick and frothy. If you can draw a line through the zabaglione with a spoon and it leaves a trail, it is ready. *Makes 2 cups (500 ml)*

Whisky sauce

Melt 2 tablespoons butter in a pan over low heat. Remove from the heat, add ¹⁄₃ cup (40 g) plain flour and stir until combined. Gradually whisk in 2 cups (500 ml) milk and 2 tablespoons caster sugar. Return to medium heat and whisk until it boils and thickens. Reduce the heat and simmer for 10 minutes, stirring occasionally. Remove from the heat, and stir in ¹⁄₃ cup (80 ml) whisky, 2 teaspoons butter and 1 tablespoon thick cream. Cover with plastic wrap until ready to serve. *Makes 2 cups (500 ml)*

Crème Anglaise

Whisk 3 egg yolks and 2 tablespoons caster sugar together in a heatproof bowl for 2 minutes, or until light and creamy. Heat 1¹⁄₂ cups (375 ml) milk until almost boiling, then pour onto the mixture, whisking constantly. Return to the clean pan and stir for 5 minutes, or until thickened enough to coat the back of a spoon. Don't allow the mixture to boil or it will curdle. Remove from the heat, stir in ¹⁄₂ teaspoon vanilla essence and transfer to a jug. Serve immediately.
Makes 2 cups (500 ml)

Vanilla custard

Combine 1 cup (250 ml) milk and ¹⁄₄ cup (60 ml) cream in a pan. Bring to the boil, then remove from the heat immediately. In a bowl, whisk 3 egg yolks, ¹⁄₂ cup (125 g) caster sugar and 2 teaspoons cornflour. Slowly pour the hot milk and cream into the egg mixture, whisking continuously. Return to the pan and stir over low heat for 5 minutes, or until thickened—do not boil. Remove from the heat and stir in ¹⁄₂ teaspoon vanilla essence. Serve immediately.
Makes 2 cups (500 ml)

SUGAR-FREE PUDDING

Preparation time: 30 minutes
Total cooking time:
    1 hour 30 minutes
Serves 6–8

6 ripe bananas, mashed
1 egg, lightly beaten
2 cups (370 g) mixed dried fruit
1 cup (80 g) fresh breadcrumbs

ORANGE CREAM
300 ml cream
2 tablespoons orange juice
1 tablespoon grated orange rind
1 teaspoon vanilla essence

1 Grease a 1.25 litre pudding basin with melted butter and place a round of baking paper in the bottom.

2 Place the basin in a large pan, on a trivet or upturned saucer, and pour in enough cold water to come halfway up the side of the basin. Remove the basin and put the water on to boil.

3 Combine the banana, egg, dried fruit and breadcrumbs in a bowl. Spoon into the prepared basin.

4 Lay a sheet of foil on the work surface and cover with a sheet of baking paper. Make a large pleat in the middle. Grease the paper with melted butter and place, paper-side-down, across the top of the basin. Tie string securely around the rim of the basin and over the top to make a handle. The handle is used to lift the pudding in and out of the pan.

5 Gently lower the basin into the boiling water, reduce the heat to a fast simmer and cover with a tight-fitting lid. Cook for 1½ hours, checking the water after an hour and topping up to the original level with boiling water as needed.

6 To make the orange cream, combine the cream, orange juice, rind and vanilla in a bowl and mix well. Serve over the pudding.

NUTRITION PER SERVE (8)
Protein 5.5 g; Fat 18 g; Carbohydrate 60 g; Dietary Fibre 5.5 g; Cholesterol 75 mg; 1720 kJ (410 cal)

NOTE: This pudding is low-fat. If you're keeping an eye on the calories, skip the orange cream.

Cover the pudding mix with a pleated layer of foil and greased baking paper.

Using the string handle, lower the pudding into boiling water.

To make the orange cream, simply combine all the ingredients in a bowl.

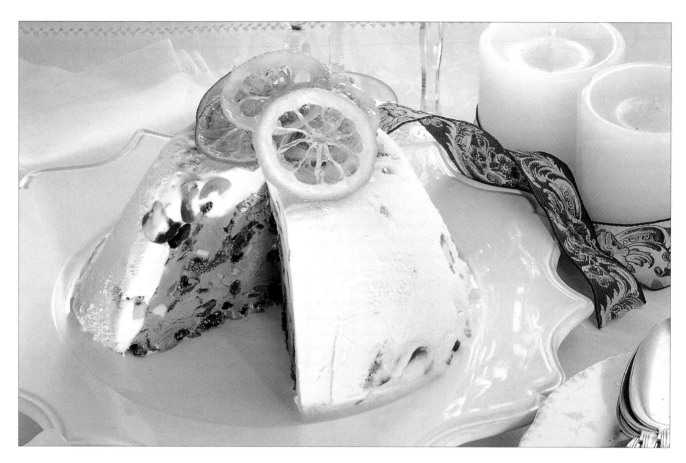

ICE CREAM CHRISTMAS PUDDING

Preparation time: 1 hour +
   overnight standing +
   2 nights freezing
Total cooking time: nil
Serves 10

1/3 cup (50 g) toasted almonds,
   chopped
1/4 cup (45 g) mixed peel
1/2 cup (60 g) raisins, chopped
1/2 cup (60 g) sultanas
1/3 cup (50 g) currants
1/3 cup (80 ml) rum
1 litre good-quality vanilla
   ice cream
1/2 cup (105 g) red and green
   glacé cherries, quartered
1 teaspoon mixed spice
1 teaspoon ground cinnamon
1/2 teaspoon ground nutmeg
1 litre good-quality chocolate
   ice cream

1 Mix the almonds, peel, raisins, sultanas, currants and rum in a bowl, cover with plastic wrap and leave overnight. Chill a 2 litre pudding basin in the freezer.

2 Soften the vanilla ice cream slightly and mix in the glacé cherries. Working quickly, press the ice cream around the inside of the chilled basin, spreading it evenly to cover the base and side of the basin. Return the basin to the freezer and leave overnight. Check the ice cream a couple of times and spread it evenly to the top.

3 The next day, mix the spices and chocolate ice cream with the fruit mixture. Spoon it into the centre of the pudding bowl and smooth the top. Freeze overnight, or until very firm. Turn the pudding out onto a chilled plate, decorate and leave to stand for 5 minutes. Cut into wedges to serve.

NUTRITION PER SERVE
Protein 7 g; Fat 25 g; Carbohydrate 45 g; Dietary Fibre 1.5 g; Cholesterol 46 mg; 1798 kJ (430 cal)

NOTE: If you want to put coins and charms into the pudding, wrap each one in baking paper and poke into the base of the pudding.

Cover the inside and base of the basin with the ice cream and cherry mixture.

Spoon the chocolate ice cream mixture into the bowl and smooth the surface.

FRESH FRUIT MINCE PIES

Preparation time: 1 hour +
    30 minutes refrigeration
Total cooking time: 50 minutes
Makes 24

PASTRY
1¾ cups (220 g) plain flour
150 g butter, chilled and
    chopped
¾ cup (80 g) ground hazelnuts
2 tablespoons caster sugar
1–2 tablespoons iced water

FILLING
¾ cup (115 g) blueberries
1 cup (200 g) peeled and
    finely chopped apple
½ cup (60 g) raisins
½ cup (75 g) currants
½ cup (60 g) sultanas
¼ cup (30 g) slivered almonds,
    toasted
¼ cup (60 g) caster sugar
2 tablespoons mixed peel
½ cup (125 ml) brandy
1 teaspoon grated lemon rind
½ teaspoon mixed spice
½ teaspoon ground ginger

1 To make the pastry, sift the flour into a large bowl and add the chopped butter. Rub the butter into the flour with your fingertips until it resembles fine breadcrumbs. Stir in the nuts and sugar. Make a well in the centre and add the water. Mix using a flat-bladed knife until the mixture comes together in beads. Gather the mixture into a ball and turn out onto a lightly floured surface. Press together into a ball and

Rub the butter into the flour with your fingertips until it resembles breadcrumbs.

Mix with a flat-bladed knife until the mixture comes together in beads.

Gather the mixture into a ball and turn out onto a lightly floured surface.

flatten slightly into a disc. Cover with plastic wrap and refrigerate for 30 minutes.

2 Preheat the oven to moderate 180°C (350°F/Gas 4). Between sheets of baking paper, roll the dough out to a 3 mm thickness. Using a 7 cm round pastry cutter, cut 24 pastry rounds and line two 12 hole deep patty pans with the rounds. Line each pastry case with baking paper and fill with baking beads. Bake for 10 minutes, remove the paper and beads and bake for a further 10 minutes.

3 Meanwhile, press together the pastry scraps and re-roll to 3 mm thickness. Using 4.5 cm star, bell or holly-shaped cutters, cut 24 shapes from the pastry for the pie lids.

4 To make the filling, place the blueberries, apple, raisins, currants, sultanas, slivered almonds, sugar, mixed peel, brandy, lemon rind, mixed spice and ground ginger in a pan and simmer, stirring well, for 5–10 minutes, or until the mixture is thick and pulpy. Spoon the filling evenly among the pastry cases, and then top each case with a pastry lid.

5 Bake the pies for 20 minutes, or until the pastry lids are golden. Leave in the tins for 5 minutes before transferring to a wire rack to cool. Dust the pies with sifted icing sugar before serving.

NUTRITION PER MINCE PIE
Protein 2 g; Fat 8 g; Carbohydrate 17 g; Dietary Fibre 1.5 g; Cholesterol 16 mg; 623 kJ (150 cal)

NOTE: Fruit mince pies will keep well for up to 7 days in an airtight container. If you prefer, they can be frozen for up to 3 months.

Line the pastry cases with baking paper and fill with baking beads.

Spoon the fruit mince filling evenly among the pastry cases.

Top the pies with a star-shaped pastry lid and bake until golden.

FRESH FRUIT PAVLOVA

Preparation time: 30 minutes
Total cooking time: 55 minutes
Serves 6–8

6 egg whites
2 cups (500 g) caster sugar
1½ tablespoons cornflour
1½ teaspoons vinegar
2 cups (500 ml) cream,
　　whipped
2 bananas, sliced
2 punnets (500 g) strawberries,
　　sliced
4 kiwi fruit, sliced
pulp from 4 passionfruit

1 Preheat the oven to slow 150°C (300°F/Gas 2). Line a large oven tray with baking paper and draw a 26 cm circle on the paper, then turn the paper over. Beat the egg whites with electric beaters in a large dry bowl until soft peaks form. Gradually add all but 2 tablespoons of the sugar, beating well after each addition. Combine the cornflour and vinegar with the last of the sugar and beat for 1 minute before adding it to the bowl. Beat for 5–10 minutes, or until all the sugar has dissolved.

2 Spread the meringue mixture onto the tray inside the circle. Shape the meringue evenly, running the flat side of a palette knife along the edge and over the top.

3 Run the palette knife up the edge of the meringue mixture all the way round, making furrows. This strengthens the pavlova and stops the edge from crumbling, as well as giving it a decorative finish.

4 Bake the meringue for 40 minutes, or until pale and crisp. Reduce the heat to very slow 120°C (250°F/Gas ½) and bake for another 15 minutes Turn off the oven and leave the pavlova inside to cool, using a wooden spoon to keep the door slightly ajar. When completely cooled, top with whipped cream and fruit. Drizzle with passionfruit pulp and serve.

NUTRITION PER SERVE (8)
Protein 6.5 g; Fat 27 g; Carbohydrate 80 g; Dietary Fibre 5 g; Cholesterol 85 mg; 2360 kJ (565 cal)

Beat the egg whites with electric beaters until soft peaks form.

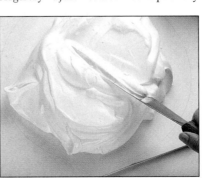

Spread the meringue mixture over the circle on the baking paper.

Use a palette knife to make furrows all around the edge of the meringue mixture.

BERRY TRIFLE

Preparation time: 35 minutes +
overnight refrigeration
Total cooking time: 5 minutes
Serves 8–10

1½ cups (2 x 225 g jars) redcurrant
    jelly
⅔ cup (170 ml) fresh orange juice
600 ml cream
250 g mascarpone
¼ cup (30 g) icing sugar
1 teaspoon vanilla essence
¼ teaspoon ground cinnamon
250 g thin sponge finger (savoiardi)
    biscuits
1½ cups (375 ml) Marsala

400 g fresh raspberries
250 g large fresh strawberries, hulled
    and quartered
400 g fresh blueberries

1 Melt the redcurrant jelly over medium heat. Remove from the heat, stir in the orange juice and set aside until the mixture reaches room temperature.

2 Place the cream, mascarpone, icing sugar, vanilla essence and cinnamon in a bowl. Using an electric mixer, whisk until soft peaks form.

3 Cut the biscuits in half and dip in the Marsala. Arrange half over the base of a 3.25 litre serving bowl.

4 Sprinkle a third of the berries over the biscuits and drizzle with half of the Marsala and a third of the redcurrant sauce. Spoon half the cream mixture over the sauce. Repeat the layering with the remaining half of the dipped biscuits and Marsala, a third of the berries and sauce, and the remaining cream.

5 Arrange the remaining berries over the cream in a mound in the centre of the bowl. Reserve the final third of the redcurrant sauce, cover and refrigerate. Cover the trifle with plastic film and refrigerate for at least 6 hours, or preferably overnight. Before serving, pour the reserved redcurrant sauce over the berries to glaze. (Gently reheat the sauce if the consistency is too thick.)

NUTRITION PER SERVE (10)
Protein 10 g; Fat 35 g; Carbohydrate 40 g; Dietary Fibre 3.5 g; Cholesterol 144 mg; 2398 kJ (575 cal)

Whisk the cream mixture with an electric beater until soft peaks form.

Pour one third of the redcurrant sauce over the layers of berries and biscuits.

Repeat the layering process with half the Marsala-dipped biscuits.

ICE CREAM BOMBE

Preparation time: 20 minutes +
overnight freezing +
25 minutes refrigeration
Total cooking time: 3 minutes
Serves 8

BOMBE
1 large mango, finely
    chopped
1 cup (160 g) canned pineapple
    pieces
¼ cup (60 ml) Grand Marnier
1²/₃ cups (250 g) fresh strawberries,
    puréed
400 g condensed milk
600 ml cream
80 g dessert nougat, chopped
    (see Note)
¼ cup (35 g) roughly chopped
    unsalted pistachio kernels
strawberries, extra, halved and
    stems intact, to garnish

TOFFEE BARK
¹/₃ cup (90 g) caster sugar

1 Line a 2 litre ceramic pudding bowl with plastic wrap, allowing it to hang over the side of the bowl. Put in the freezer until ready to use. Drain the mango and pineapple in a sieve.

2 Mix together the Grand Marnier, strawberry purée and condensed milk. Whisk the cream to soft peaks, then add to the condensed milk mixture and continue whisking until thick. Fold in the drained fruits, nougat and pistachio kernels. Pour the mixture into the pudding bowl, cover with plastic wrap and freeze overnight, or until firm.

3 To serve, remove the plastic wrap from the base and invert the pudding onto a chilled serving plate. Remove the pudding bowl, but leave the plastic wrap and refrigerate for 15–25 minutes to soften.

4 To make the toffee bark, line an oven tray with baking paper. Heat the sugar over gentle heat in a heavy-based pan for 4–5 minutes, or until melted and golden. Carefully pour onto the prepared tray. Tilt the tray to get a thin, even layer of toffee over

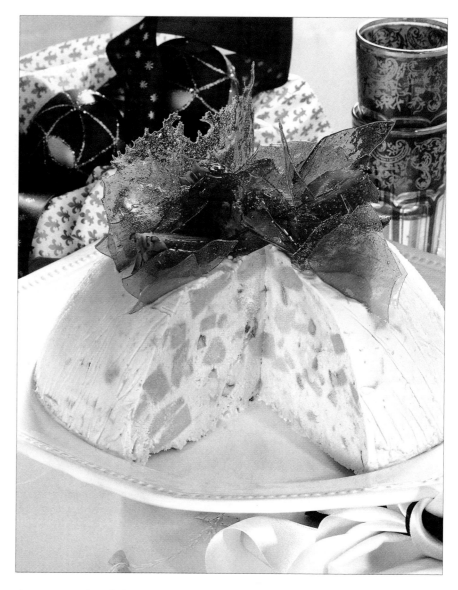

the paper and cool slightly. While still pliable, drape the paper over a rolling pin and cool for 30–60 seconds before peeling away strips of toffee in large irregular shapes. Cool. To serve, remove the plastic wrap and decorate the bombe with toffee bark and extra strawberries.

NUTRITION PER SERVE
Protein 8 g; Fat 40 g; Carbohydrate 56 g; Dietary Fibre 2 g; Cholesterol 120 mg; 2595 kJ (620 cal)

NOTE: Dessert nougat a soft nougat available from confectionery shops and delicatessens.

Drape the toffee-coated baking paper over a rolling pin and allow to set.

Peel the toffee bark away from the paper in large, irregular shapes.

BERRIES IN CHAMPAGNE JELLY

Preparation time: 10 minutes
+ refrigeration
Total cooking time: 5 minutes
Serves 8

1 litre Champagne or sparkling
    white wine
1½ tablespoons gelatine
1 cup (250 g) sugar
4 strips lemon rind
4 strips orange rind
1⅔ cups (250 g) small fresh
    strawberries, hulled
1⅔ cups (255 g) fresh blueberries

1 Pour 2 cups (500 ml) Champagne or sparkling white wine into a bowl and let the bubbles subside.

Sprinkle the gelatine over the Champagne in an even layer. Leave until the gelatine is spongy—do not stir. Place the remaining Champagne in a large pan with the sugar, lemon and orange rind, and heat gently, stirring constantly, until all the sugar has dissolved.

2 Remove the pan from the heat, add the gelatine mixture and stir until thoroughly dissolved. Leave the jelly to cool completely, then remove the lemon and orange rind.

3 Divide the strawberries and blueberries among eight ½ cup (125 ml) stemmed wine glasses (or eight small glass bowls) and gently pour the jelly over them. Refrigerate until the jelly has fully set. Take the jellies out of the refrigerator at least 15 minutes before serving.

NUTRITION PER SERVE
Protein 3 g; Fat 0 g; Carbohydrate 37 g;
Dietary Fibre 1.5 g; Cholesterol 0 mg;
965 kJ (230 cal)

Sprinkle the gelatine over the Champagne in an even layer and leave until spongy.

Pour the jelly into the wine glasses, covering the berries.

YULE LOG

Preparation time: 40 minutes
Total cooking time: 15 minutes
Serves 8

½ cup (60 g) plain flour
2 tablespoons cocoa powder
3 eggs
⅓ cup (90 g) caster sugar
50 g butter, melted and cooled
1 tablespoon caster sugar, extra

FILLING
125 g white chocolate, chopped
½ cup (125 ml) cream
50 g hazelnuts, toasted and
    finely chopped

TOPPING
125 g dark chocolate, chopped
½ cup (125 ml) cream
icing sugar, to dust

1 Brush a 30 x 35 cm Swiss roll tin with oil or melted butter and line the base and sides with baking paper. Preheat the oven to moderate 180°C (350°F/Gas 4). Sift the flour and cocoa powder together twice. Using electric beaters, beat the eggs and sugar for 5 minutes, or until light and fluffy and increased in volume.

2 Sift the flour mixture over the eggs and pour the butter around the edge of the bowl. Using a large metal spoon, gently fold the mixture together to incorporate the flour and butter. Take care not to overmix and lose too much volume.

3 Spread the mixture into the prepared tin and bake for about 12 minutes, or until the sponge springs back to the light touch. Sprinkle the extra caster sugar over a clean tea towel. Turn the sponge out onto the tea towel, close to one end. Roll up the sponge and tea towel together lengthways, and leave to cool completely.

4 To make the filling, put the white chocolate in a small heatproof bowl. Bring a small pan of water to the boil, then remove from the heat. Add the cream to the chocolate and stand the bowl over the pan of water, making sure the base of the bowl does not touch the water, until the chocolate is soft. Stir until smooth. Repeat with the dark chocolate and cream for the topping. Leave the white chocolate mixture until it has cooled to room temperature and is the consistency of cream. Leave the dark chocolate mixture until it cools to a spreadable consistency.

5 Using electric beaters, beat the white chocolate mixture until soft peaks form—do not overbeat. Unroll the sponge, remove the tea towel and paper and spread with the filling, finishing 2 cm from the end. Sprinkle with the hazelnuts. Re-roll the sponge, and trim the ends. Cut one end off on the diagonal and place it alongside the log to create a branch.

6 Place the roll onto a serving plate, and spread the dark chocolate topping all over it. Run the tines of a fork along the length of the roll, to give a 'bark' effect. Just before serving, dust generously with icing sugar. Decorate with some fresh green leaves.

NUTRITION PER SERVE
Protein 8 g; Fat 35 g; Carbohydrate 45 g; Dietary Fibre 1.5 g; Cholesterol 130 mg; 2072 kJ (495 cal)

NOTE: Keep, covered in plastic wrap, in the refrigerator for 4–5 days.

Using electric beaters, beat the eggs and sugar until light and fluffy.

Pour the sponge mixture into the prepared tin and spread evenly.

Roll the sponge up lengthways in a tea towel and leave to cool.

Melt the white chocolate and add the cream, stirring until smooth.

Unroll the sponge and spread with the filling, leaving a 2 cm border.

Use a fork to make a 'bark' effect on the log topping.

CHRISTMAS CAKE

Preparation time: 40 minutes
+ overnight soaking
Total cooking time:
3 hours 40 minutes
Serves 20

250 g sultanas
250 g raisins
300 g currants
200 g mixed peel
100 g whole red glacé cherries
100 g glacé (cooking) ginger,
    roughly chopped
150 g chopped glacé apricots
½ cup (125 ml) brandy
½ cup (125 ml) orange juice
1½ cups (185 g) walnuts
250 g butter, chopped and at
    room temperature
1 cup (230 g) firmly packed soft
    brown sugar
½ cup (160 g) orange
    marmalade
5 eggs
2 cups (250 g) plain flour
1 teaspoon bicarbonate of soda
1 teaspoon ground cinnamon
1 teaspoon nutmeg

1 Combine all the fruit in a large bowl, working with your fingers to separate any lumps. Add the brandy and orange juice, and stir well. Cover with plastic wrap and leave overnight (or for at least 4 hours) for the fruit to absorb most of the liquid, stirring occasionally.

2 Preheat the oven to warm 160°C (315°F/Gas 2–3). Brush a 23 cm round or square cake tin with oil or melted butter. Cut 2 strips of baking paper, long enough to fit around the sides of the tin in one piece and tall enough to come 5 cm above the top edge. Fold down a cuff about 2 cm deep along the length of each strip. Make diagonal cuts up to the fold line on each strip, approximately 1 cm apart. Fit the strips around the inside of the tin, pressing the cuts so they fit flat around the bottom edge of the tin. Cut 2 pieces of paper to fit the base of the tin and place in the base of the tin.

3 Put the walnuts on a baking tray and place into the preheated oven for about 8–10 minutes (watch to make sure they don't burn), or until fragrant and lightly toasted. Cool and roughly chop.

4 Using electric beaters, beat the butter, sugar and marmalade in a large bowl until light and creamy. Scrape down the sides of the bowl with a rubber spatula. Add the eggs one at a time, beating well after each addition. The mixture will appear curdled but don't worry.

5 Add the butter mixture and the walnuts to the soaked fruit. Sift the flour and spices on top, then mix together gently but thoroughly. Make sure there are no pockets of flour in the mixture, but do not beat too vigorously.

6 Spoon the mixture into the prepared tin, then wrap the outside of the tin with a double thickness of newspaper, and secure with string. Bake for 3–3½ hours, or until a skewer inserted into the centre of the cake comes out clean and the cake has shrunk slightly from the edge of the tin. Cool in the tin before turning it out.

NUTRITION PER SERVE
Protein 6 g; Fat 18 g; Carbohydrate 65 g; Dietary Fibre 3.5 g; Cholesterol 75 mg; 1910 kJ (457 cal)

Add the brandy and orange juice to the fruit mixture and stir well.

Make diagonal cuts along the 2 cm cuff folded in the baking paper strips.

Fit the baking paper strips inside the tin so that they fit around the bottom.

The mixture appears curdled after the eggs are added but don't worry.

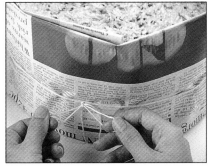

Wrap a double thickness of newspaper around the tin and tie securely with string.

The cake is cooked when a metal skewer inserted into the centre comes out clean.

ICING YOUR CAKE

A beautifully decorated Christmas cake doesn't have to be beyond you. Decorating your cake will be a lot easier if you follow these instructions, and the best part is you can do it up to a month before Christmas.

ONCE YOU have cooked your Christmas cake, it is time to decorate it. Firstly you must cover the cake with marzipan. Then you have a choice between ready-made soft icing or, if you want to be a little more adventurous, royal icing. You can also add handmade decorations such as Christmas trees, presents, holly leaves or Christmas messages. The icing amounts given here will cover a 23 cm cake, such as the Christmas cake on page 62.

MARZIPAN ICING

To make marzipan icing, you will need 2 tablespoons apricot jam and 800 g marzipan or almond icing.

1 Trim the dome from the cake to give it a flat surface and turn it upside-down on a board which is

Fill any holes in the surface of the cake with rolled-up balls of marzipan.

Brush the melted jam all over the surface of the cake with a pastry brush.

Drape the marzipan over a rolling pin and move it carefully onto the cake.

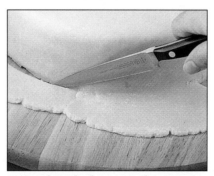

Use a sharp knife to trim the marzipan around the base of the cake.

4 cm larger than the cake. Fill any holes in the surface of the cake with small pieces of marzipan. Heat the jam in a small pan with 1 teaspoon water, then push it through a fine sieve and brush it all over the cake with a pastry brush.

2 Briefly knead the marzipan on a clean work surface dusted lightly with icing sugar until it is smooth. Roll it out to a circle large enough to just cover the base and side of the cake—don't roll it out too big or you may get folds in it.

3 Drape the marzipan over a rolling pin lightly dusted with icing sugar, then carefully lift it over the cake and unroll it onto the cake, smoothing it over the base and side and pressing out any folds and wrinkles with icing sugar-dusted hands. Carefully pierce

any air bubbles with a pin. Trim the marzipan around the base of the cake with a sharp knife and leave the cake in a cool, dry place overnight.

SOFT ICING

To make soft icing, you will need 1 egg white and 1 kg ready-made soft icing.

1 Lightly beat the egg white in a clean, dry bowl and then brush it all over the surface of the marzipan in a thin layer. (This will help the icing stick to the marzipan.)

2 Briefly knead the icing on a clean work surface, lightly dusted with icing sugar, until it is smooth and pliable. Roll it out just large enough to cover the cake, dusting your rolling pin and bench with more icing sugar if needed.

3 Roll the icing over the rolling pin and drape it carefully over the cake, gently pressing the icing over the cake. Dust your hands with icing sugar and smooth out any wrinkles and folds. You can also use a 'smoother' available from cake decorating shops. Or, make your own smoother with a smooth-edged piece of laminex and a wooden block glued to the back as a handle. Trim the icing around the base of the cake with a sharp knife and leave the cake in a cool, dry place overnight.

Press the soft icing over the cake and smooth out any wrinkles or folds.

ROYAL ICING

To make royal icing, you will need 500 g pure icing sugar and 3 lightly beaten egg whites.

1 Sift the icing sugar into a large bowl and make a well in the centre, add the egg whites and gradually incorporate them into the icing sugar, stirring from the centre outwards until everything is completely mixed in. The mixture will be fairly stiff. Beat it with an electric hand mixer until it is fluffy—the mixture should be spreadable but not runny.

2 Icing your cake is much easier if you have a turntable. If not, place your cake on an upturned cake tin to give you a little bit more height and

Spoon a third of the royal icing onto the cake and smooth out with a palette knife.

Pull the palette knife over the surface of the cake to smooth the icing out.

Use the palette knife to create a snow scene on the surface of the cake.

make turning the cake easier. Spoon about a third of the icing onto the surface of the marzipan-covered cake and spread it out to the edge of the cake with a palette knife. If you have one, use a steel ruler to smooth the surface; if not use the palette knife. Hold each end of the palette knife and pull it towards you over the icing (you may need to do this a few times, adding more icing as necessary). Ice the side of the cake and when you have a surface that is as smooth as possible, leave the cake to dry. (If you want to create a snow scene, press down with a palette knife and lift at intervals all over the icing to make peaks, and then leave to dry.)

ICING DECORATIONS

To make your icing decorations you will need ready-made soft icing, icing sugar, assorted food colourings and thin ribbons, if desired.

Christmas trees: Colour various sized pieces of icing green and roll them into cone shapes. Use a pair of scissors to make snips into the side of the cone all over. Leave to dry. Cut small stars out of yellow tinted icing and leave to dry. Stick the stars to the top of the tree with some royal icing. Dust with sifted icing sugar.

Presents: Make little shapes of icing in varying sizes and leave them to dry. Paint each one in a different colour and leave to dry. Then paint bows and ribbons, stripes and spots on the presents in different colours. Arrange a selection of decorations on your cake, attaching them with a little royal icing. You can also tie a ribbon or frill around the cake and, if you wish, write a Christmas greeting.

Runout letters: Trace a Christmas greeting from a lettering book or Christmas card onto a piece of paper in simple, easy-to-read letters. Place the paper on a board and cover with a piece of baking paper. Make up some icing using an egg white and enough pure icing sugar to make a smooth icing which will hold its shape. Tint with colour and spoon it into a paper piping bag. Pipe around the outline of the letters and then fill in the centre. If the icing is too stiff and doesn't sit flat, brush it with a paint brush dipped in egg white. Leave to dry overnight and then very carefully peel the letters off the

Make Christmas tree decorations out of green coloured icing.

Paint small pieces of icing different colours to make presents.

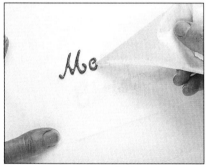

Write your greeting on baking paper and attach to the cake when dry.

paper and stick them to the cake with a little royal icing.

Leaves: Use a holly-shaped cutter to cut leaves out of the icing. Shape the leaves and leave to dry. When dry, paint the leaves green. Roll small amounts of icing into balls to represent holly berries. Paint the balls red and leave to dry. Holly leaves can also be used alone as a border around the edge of the cake to represent a wreath.

NOTE: Never use real holly berries to decorate your cake—they are toxic!

STORAGE: Keep your iced and decorated Christmas cake in an airtight container in a cool, dry place for 4–5 months. Do not refrigerate or the icing will go sticky.

BOILED FRUIT CAKE

Preparation time: 20 minutes
Total cooking time:
    2 hours 10 minutes
Serves 16–18

2 cups (250 g) raisins
2 cups (250 g) sultanas
1 cup (150 g) currants
2/3 cup (100 g) blanched
    almonds, chopped
100 g red glacé cherries
1 cup (230 g) firmly packed
    soft brown sugar
125 g butter, chopped
1/4 cup (80 ml) brandy
2 eggs, lightly beaten
3/4 cup (90 g) plain flour
3/4 cup (90 g) self-raising
    flour
1 tablespoon mixed spice

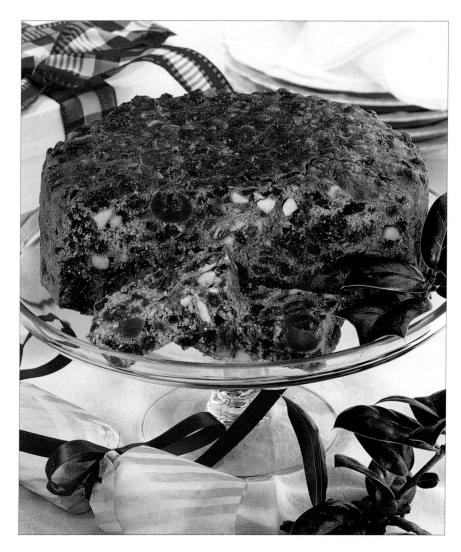

1 Combine all the dried fruits, almonds, glacé cherries, sugar, butter, brandy and 1 cup (250 ml) water in a large pan. Bring to the boil (stir occasionally to ensure the sugar dissolves and butter melts evenly through the mixture), then remove from the heat and cool.

2 Preheat the oven to warm 160°C (315°F/Gas 2–3). Brush the base and side of a 20 cm round tin with oil or melted butter. Cut 2 strips of baking paper long enough to fit around the outside of the tin and tall enough to come 5 cm above the top edge. Fold down a cuff about 2 cm deep along the length of each strip. Make diagonal cuts up to the fold line on each strip approximately 1 cm apart. Fit the strips around the inside of the tin, pressing the cuts so they sit flat around the bottom edge of the tin. Cut 2 circles of baking paper, using the tin as your guide. Place the two circles of baking paper into the base of the tin.

3 Add the eggs to the mixture, then sift in the flours and mixed spice. Mix together thoroughly, working quickly and lightly—don't beat vigorously. Pour the mixture into the prepared tin, smooth the top of the cake with wetted hands and bake for 1 1/2–2 hours, or until a skewer inserted into the centre of the cake comes out clean. Cool completely in the tin, then turn out.

NUTRITION PER SERVE (18)
Protein 4 g; Fat 9.5 g; Carbohydrate 45 g; Dietary Fibre 2.5 g; Cholesterol 40 mg; 1186 kJ (285 cal)

Stir to ensure the sugar dissolves and butter melts evenly through the mixture.

Add the eggs, flours and mixed spice and mix thoroughly.

Smooth over the top of the cake with wetted hands before baking.

LIGHT FRUIT CAKE

Preparation time: 20 minutes
Total cooking time:
    1 hour 40 minutes
Serves 16–18

250 g butter, chopped and
    at room temperature
1 cup (250 g) caster sugar
4 eggs
1 teaspoon vanilla essence
2 cups (250 g) self-raising
    flour
1/2 cup (60 g) plain flour
1 teaspoon mixed spice
500 g mixed dried fruit
1/2 cup (125 ml) milk

1 Preheat the oven to moderate 180°C (350°F/Gas 4). Brush a 20 cm round tin with oil or melted butter. Cut 2 strips of baking paper long enough to fit around the outside of the tin and tall enough to come 5 cm above the top edge. Fold down a cuff about 2 cm deep along the length of each strip. Make diagonal cuts up to the fold line on each strip approximately 1 cm apart. Fit the strips around the inside of the tin, pressing the cuts so they sit flat around the bottom edge of the tin. Cut two circles of baking paper, using the tin as a guide, and place the circles in the base of the tin.

2 Using electric beaters, beat the butter and sugar together until light and creamy. Add the eggs one at a time, beating well after each addition. Add the vanilla essence and beat the mixture until combined. The mixture will appear curdled at this stage but this is fine.

3 Sift the flours and mixed spice together in a bowl, add the dried fruit and toss to coat with the flour, separating any clumps of fruit with your fingers. Add to the butter mixture, with the milk, and mix gently until combined. Transfer to the prepared tin. Tap the base gently to release any air bubbles.

4 Bake for 1 hour 40 minutes, or until a skewer inserted into the centre of the cake comes out clean and the cake has shrunk slightly from the edge of the tin. Leave in the tin for 15 minutes, then turn out onto a wire rack to cool.

NUTRITION PER SERVE (18)
Protein 4.5 g; Fat 13 g; Carbohydrate 47 g; Dietary Fibre 2.5 g; Cholesterol 75 mg; 1335 kJ (320 cal)

Using electric beaters, beat the butter and sugar together until light and creamy.

Coat the fruit in the flour and spice, separating any clumps with your fingers.

CHOCOLATE MOUSSE TORTE WITH RASPBERRY FILLING

Preparation time: 1 hour +
3 hours refrigeration
Total cooking time: 50 minutes
Serves 10–12

BOTTOM LAYER
2 cups (250 g) chopped walnuts
200 g butter, chopped
3/4 cup (185 g) caster sugar
4 eggs, separated
200 g dark chocolate, melted
and cooled
300 g fresh raspberries, or
frozen raspberries, thawed
and drained

TOP LAYER
2 eggs
1/4 cup (60 g) sugar
200 g white chocolate, melted
and cooled
250 g mascarpone cheese
2 tablespoons Grand Marnier
2 tablespoons orange juice
2 teaspoons gelatine
1 cup (250 ml) cream, whipped

cocoa powder, to decorate
150 g dark chocolate melts

1 Preheat the oven to moderate 180°C (350°F/Gas 4). Spread the walnuts onto a tray and bake for about 8–10 minutes, or until fragrant and lightly toasted (make sure they don't burn). Cool, then place in a food processor and process until finely ground. Brush a round 22 cm springform tin with melted butter and line the base and side with baking paper.

2 Using electric beaters, beat the butter and sugar until light and creamy. Add the egg yolks one at a time, beating well after each addition. Add the chocolate and beat until combined. Stir the ground walnuts into the mixture.

3 Using clean beaters, beat the egg whites in a clean, dry bowl until soft peaks form. Fold a quarter of the beaten egg white into the chocolate mixture, then gently fold in the remainder. Work carefully, so there are no white streaks in the mixture, but without losing too much volume. Spoon into the prepared tin, and bake for 35–40 minutes, or until the side of the cake has risen and the top has a crust (the centre will still be soft). Leave to cool, then refrigerate for about 1 hour, or until firm. The centre of the cake will sink on cooling, which is fine.

4 Remove the cake from the tin and peel the paper from the side. Invert onto a flat serving plate and remove the paper from the base. Put the cleaned ring part of the tin back around the cake (not the base). Sprinkle the raspberries over the top of the cake, leaving a gap of about 1 cm around the edge.

5 To make the top layer, beat the eggs and sugar until thick and pale and increased in volume. On low speed, beat in the chocolate, mascarpone and Grand Marnier until combined (don't overbeat). Place the orange juice in a bowl and sprinkle on the gelatine in an even layer. Leave until the gelatine is spongy—do not stir. Bring a small pan of water to the boil, remove from the heat and

place the bowl in the pan. The water should come halfway up the sides of the bowl. Stir the gelatine until clear and dissolved. Allow to cool slightly. Stir into the chocolate mixture, then gently fold in the whipped cream.

6 Spoon the mousse onto the cooled cake base, covering the raspberries and making sure it reaches right to

Fold the beaten egg white through the chocolate, making sure there are no streaks.

Sprinkle the raspberries over the top of the cake, leaving a gap around the edge.

Cover the raspberries with the white chocolate mousse mixture.

the side of the tin. Smooth the surface as much as is possible. Refrigerate for 2 hours, or until set.

7 Run a flat-bladed knife around the inside of the tin. Cut a large star shape from a piece of cardboard and use as a stencil over the cake, resting the cardboard over the tin and dusting generously with cocoa, to make a big chocolate star on the top. Carefully remove the tin.

8 Cut a piece of glossy contact or baking paper as wide as the tin is high, and long enough to fit around the cake. Melt the chocolate melts, cool slightly, and spread over the paper, right up to the edges. Wrap the paper carefully around the cake, chocolate side against the cake, before the chocolate sets. Leave for the chocolate to set. When set, gently peel away the paper. Serve.

NUTRITION PER SERVE (12)
Protein 13 g; Fat 55 g; Carbohydrate 45 g; Dietary Fibre 3 g; Cholesterol 170 mg; 717 kJ (170 cal)

Make a star on the top of the cake using cocoa and a cardboard stencil.

Spread the slightly cooled melted chocolate evenly over the contact.

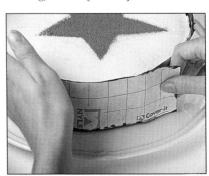

Wrap the chocolate around the side of the cake and remove the contact when set.

GLACE FRUIT AND NUT LOAF

Preparation time: 30 minutes
Total cooking time:
    1 hour 45 minutes
Serves 12

50 g butter, softened
¼ cup (55 g) firmly packed
    soft brown sugar
2 tablespoons breakfast marmalade
2 eggs
1 cup (125 g) plain flour
1 teaspoon baking powder
1 teaspoon ground nutmeg
1¼ cups (225 g) pitted dates
1½ cups (185 g) raisins
1 cup (155 g) brazil nuts
⅔ cup (140 g) red, yellow and green
    glacé cherries
½ cup (110 g) chopped glacé
    pear or pineapple
½ cup (120 g) chopped glacé
    apricots
½ cup (120 g) chopped glacé
    peaches
⅓ cup (120 g) chopped glacé figs
1 cup (100 g) walnut halves
⅔ cup (100 g) blanched almonds

TOPPING
2 teaspoons gelatine
2 tablespoons breakfast marmalade
150 g glacé pineapple or pear rings
100 g red, yellow and green
    glacé cherries
¼ cup (40 g) blanched almonds,
    toasted

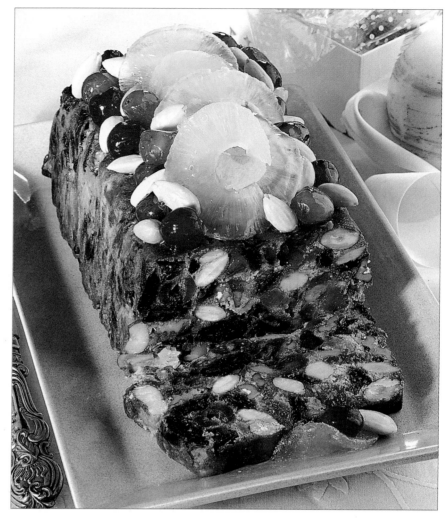

1 Grease a 20.5 x 8 x 7 cm bar tin and line the base and sides with baking paper. Preheat the oven to slow 150°C (300°F/Gas 2).

2 Place the butter, sugar and marmalade in a bowl and mix together until pale and creamy. Add the eggs and beat until combined.

3 Sift the flour, baking powder and nutmeg into a large bowl. Add the fruit and nuts and mix together until each piece is coated in the flour mixture. Add to the egg mixture and combine well.

4 Put the mixture in the prepared tin, pushing well into each corner. Bake for 1½–1¾ hours, or until a skewer inserted into the centre comes out clean. Cool in the tin for 10 minutes before turning out. Remove the baking paper and transfer to a wire rack to cool.

5 For the topping, sprinkle the gelatine over the marmalade and 2 tablespoons water in a small bowl. Bring a pan of water to the boil, then remove from the heat. Stand the bowl in the pan and stir until the gelatine has dissolved. Brush the top of the cake with some of the gelatine mixture, and arrange the pineapple, cherries and almonds over the top. Brush or drizzle with more gelatine mixture and allow to set.

NUTRITION PER SERVE
Protein 9 g; Fat 25 g; Carbohydrate 87 g; Dietary Fibre 6 g; Cholesterol 40 mg; 2496 kJ (596 cal)

Coat the fruit and nuts in the flour mixture before adding to the egg mixture.

Drizzle extra gelatine over the glacé fruit and nut topping and allow to set.

STOLLEN

Preparation time: 30 minutes +
1 hour 45 minutes proving
Total cooking time: 40 minutes
Serves 6–8

1/3 cup (80 ml) lukewarm water
1/3 cup (80 ml) lukewarm milk
2 teaspoons sugar
7 g sachet dried yeast
120 g butter, softened
1/3 cup (90 g) caster sugar
1 egg
2 teaspoons vanilla essence
1/2 teaspoon ground cinnamon
3 cups (375 g) plain flour
1/2 cup (60 g) raisins
1/2 cup (75 g) currants
1/2 cup (95 g) mixed peel
1/2 cup (60 g) slivered almonds
30 g butter, melted
icing sugar, to dust

1 Combine the water, milk, sugar and yeast in a small bowl. Stand in a warm place for 10 minutes, or until the mixture is foamy. Meanwhile, beat the butter and sugar with electric beaters until light and creamy, then beat in the egg and vanilla essence.

2 Add the foamy yeast mixture, cinnamon and almost all the flour and mix to a soft dough, adding more flour if necessary. Turn out onto a lightly floured surface and knead for 10 minutes, or until the dough is smooth and elastic. Place in a lightly oiled bowl, cover with plastic wrap and leave for 1 hour 45 minutes in a warm place, or until doubled in volume. Preheat the oven to moderate 180°C (350°F/Gas 4). Brush an oven tray lightly with oil or melted butter.

3 When the dough has risen, tip it out of the bowl onto a floured work surface and punch it to expel the air and then press it out to a thickness of about 1.5 cm. Sprinkle the fruit and nuts over the dough, then gather up and knead for a few minutes to mix the fruit and nuts evenly through the dough.

4 Shape the dough into an oval about 18 cm wide and 30 cm long. Fold in half lengthways, and press down to flatten slightly, with the fold slightly off centre on top of the loaf. Place on the prepared tray, and bake for 40 minutes, or until golden brown. As soon as it comes out of the oven, brush the loaf with the melted butter, allowing each brushing to be absorbed until you have used all the butter up. Cool on a wire rack. Dust with icing sugar before cutting to serve.

NUTRITION PER SERVE (8)
Protein 9.5 g; Fat 20 g; Carbohydrate 57 g; Dietary Fibre 4.5 g; Cholesterol 72 mg; 1905 kJ (455 cal)

Sprinkle the fruit and nuts over the dough and knead to mix through evenly.

Fold the dough in half lengthways, with the fold on top, and flatten slightly.

PARTIES

EVERYONE LOVES a party—and Christmas is definitely party time. Office parties, family reunions, drinks with old friends, any excuse to spread a little festive spirit! Planning your Christmas celebration doesn't have to be a drama-ridden nightmare. A little organisation, and a delicious selection of finger food, fresh seafood and warm or chilled cocktails will have everyone revelling in festive cheer. You never know, you may even get to relax and enjoy yourself too!

BLUE CHEESE AND PORT PATE

Preparation time: 10 minutes + refrigeration
Total cooking time: nil
Serves 8

350 g cream cheese,
    at room temperature
60 g unsalted butter,
    softened
1/3 cup (80 ml) port
300 g blue cheese,
    at room temperature,
    mashed
1 tablespoon snipped
    fresh chives
45 g walnut halves

1 Using electric beaters, beat the cream cheese and butter until smooth, then stir in the port. Add the blue cheese and chives and stir until just combined. Season to taste.
2 Spoon the mixture into a serving bowl and smooth the surface. Cover the pâté with plastic wrap and refrigerate until firm.

3 Arrange the walnuts over the top, pressing down lightly. Serve at room temperature with crusty bread, crackers and celery sticks.

NUTRITION PER SERVE
Protein 12 g; Fat 37 g; Carbohydrate 2.5 g; Dietary Fibre 0.5 g; Cholesterol 100 mg; 1650 kJ (395 cal)

Stir the blue cheese and chives into the cream cheese and butter mixture.

Arrange the walnut halves over the surface, pressing down lightly.

CHICKEN LIVER AND GRAND MARNIER PATE

Preparation time: 20 minutes + soaking and refrigeration
Total cooking time: 10 minutes
Serves 8

750 g chicken livers, trimmed
1 cup (250 ml) milk
200 g butter, softened
½ cup (60 g) finely chopped spring onions
1 tablespoon Grand Marnier
1 tablespoon frozen orange juice concentrate, thawed
½ orange, very thinly sliced

JELLIED LAYER
1 tablespoon frozen orange juice concentrate, thawed
1 tablespoon Grand Marnier
1¼ cups (315 ml) canned chicken consommé, undiluted
2½ teaspoons gelatine

1 Place the chicken livers in a large bowl, add the milk and stir to combine. Cover and refrigerate for 1 hour. Drain the livers and discard the milk. Rinse well in cold water, drain and pat dry with paper towels.

2 Melt a third of the butter in a frying pan, add the spring onion and cook for 2–3 minutes, or until tender, but not brown. Add the chicken livers and cook, stirring, over medium heat for 4–5 minutes, or until just cooked. Remove from the heat and cool a little.

3 Place the contents of the pan in a food processor and process until very smooth. Chop the remaining butter, and add to the food processor with the Grand Marnier and orange concentrate. Process until creamy and season. Place the pâté in a 1.25 litre serving dish, cover the surface of the pâté with plastic wrap and refrigerate for 1½ hours, or until firm.

4 To make the jellied layer, whisk the orange juice concentrate, Grand Marnier and ½ cup (125 ml) of the consommé together in a bowl, and sprinkle on the gelatine in an even layer. Set aside and leave until the gelatine is spongy—do not stir. Heat the remaining consommé, then remove from the heat and add the gelatine mixture to the pan. Stir gently to dissolve the gelatine and leave to cool and thicken until the mixture is the consistency of an uncooked egg white.

5 Press the orange slices lightly into the surface of the pâté and spoon the thickened jelly over the top. Refrigerate until set. Serve at room temperature with toast or crackers.

NUTRITION PER SERVE
Protein 20 g; Fat 25 g; Carbohydrate 8 g; Dietary Fibre 0 g; Cholesterol 260 mg; 1480 kJ (355 cal)

Cook the spring onion and chicken livers over medium heat until just cooked.

Blend the chicken liver mixture in a food processor until creamy.

Add the gelatine mixture to the heated consommé, then leave to cool and thicken.

SEAFOOD TERRINE

Preparation time: 1 hour + cooling
and refrigeration
Total cooking time: 50 minutes
Serves 8

FIRST LAYER
500 g raw prawns, chilled
2 egg whites, chilled
freshly grated nutmeg, to taste
220 ml cream, chilled
150 g baby green beans

SECOND LAYER
250 g salmon fillet without skin
and bones, chopped
2 egg whites, chilled
2 tablespoons chopped
fresh chives
220 ml cream, chilled

TOMATO COULIS
2 tablespoons extra virgin olive oil
1 onion, very finely chopped
750 g ripe Roma tomatoes, peeled,
seeded and diced
2 tablespoons Grand Marnier,
optional

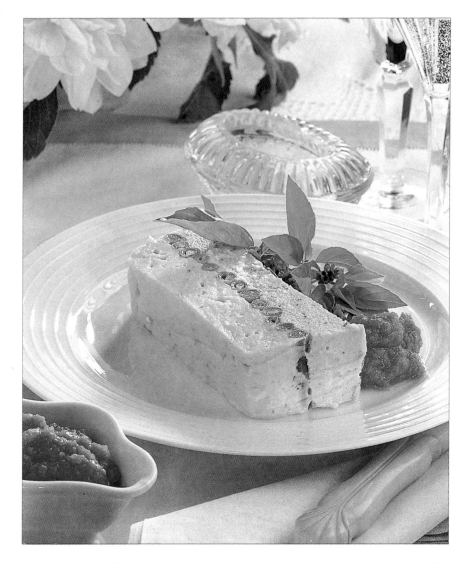

1 Preheat the oven to moderate 180°C (350°F/Gas 4). Brush a 1.5 litre (22 x 12 cm) loaf tin with oil and line the base with baking paper. To make the first layer, peel and devein the prawns and finely chop in a food processor. Add the egg whites one at a time, processing until smooth. Season with salt, pepper and nutmeg. Add the cream slowly and then stop the machine. Spoon into the tin, cover and refrigerate.

2 Cook the beans in boiling water until tender, then drain and plunge into cold water. Drain again and dry with paper towels. Arrange lengthways over the prawn mixture.

3 To make the second layer, process the salmon until finely chopped. Add the egg whites one at a time and process until smooth, then add the chives. Add the cream slowly and then stop the machine. Spread evenly over the beans.

4 Cover the loaf tin tightly with foil brushed with oil and place in a baking dish. Pour cold water into the dish to come halfway up the sides of the tin. Bake for 35 minutes, or until lightly set in the centre. Leave to cool before removing the foil. Cover with plastic wrap and refrigerate until firm. Serve at room temperature.

5 To make the coulis, heat the oil in a pan, add the onion and cook over medium heat for 5 minutes, or until soft. Add the tomato and Grand Marnier and bring to the boil. Boil for 8 minutes, or until thickened slightly. Cool, then process until smooth. Season to taste and serve with slices of the terrine.

NUTRITION PER SERVE
Protein 22.5 g; Fat 33 g; Carbohydrate 7 g; Dietary Fibre 2 g; Cholesterol 190 mg; 1749 kJ (415 cal)

Spread the second layer evenly over the beans, smoothing with the back of a spoon.

Boil the tomato coulis until it has thickened slightly.

GRAVADLAX

Preparation time: 20 minutes +
    overnight refrigeration
Total cooking time: nil
Serves 20

3 tablespoons sugar
2 tablespoons coarse sea salt
1 teaspoon crushed black
    peppercorns
1 x 2.5 kg salmon, filleted and
    deboned but with the skin left
    on
    (ask your fishmonger to do this)
1 tablespoon vodka or brandy
4 tablespoons very finely
    chopped fresh dill

MUSTARD SAUCE
1½ tablespoons cider vinegar
1 teaspoon caster sugar
½ cup (125 ml) olive oil
2 teaspoons chopped fresh dill
2 tablespoons Dijon mustard

1 Combine the sugar, salt and peppercorns in a small dish. Remove any bones from the salmon fillets. Pat dry with paper towels and lay one fillet skin-side-down in a shallow tray or baking dish. Sprinkle with half the vodka or brandy and rub half the sugar mixture into the flesh, then sprinkle on half the dill. Sprinkle the remaining vodka over the second salmon fillet and rub the remaining sugar mixture into the flesh. Lay it flesh-side-down on top of the dill-coated salmon. Cover with plastic wrap and place a heavy board on top, then weigh this down with 3 heavy cans or a foil-covered brick.

2 Place the wrapped salmon in the refrigerator for 24 hours, turning it over after 12 hours.

3 To make the mustard sauce, whisk together the ingredients, then cover until needed.

4 When the salmon is ready, take off the weights and remove the plastic wrap. Lift off the top fillet and lay both fillets on a wooden board. Brush off all the dill and any seasoning mixture with a stiff pastry brush. Sprinkle with the remaining fresh dill and press it onto the salmon flesh, shaking off any excess.

5 Serve whole on the serving board or very thinly sliced on an angle towards the tail, with the sauce.

NUTRITION PER SERVE
Protein 22.5 g; Fat 15 g; Carbohydrate 3 g; Dietary Fibre 0 g; Cholesterol 37.5 mg; 1234 kJ (294 cal)

Rub the sugar mixture into the second salmon fillet.

Whisk all the ingredients of the mustard sauce together.

The salmon can be served sliced thinly on an angle towards the tail.

SEAFOOD TREATS

Melt-in-the-mouth delicious, shellfish are one of nature's delights. And you can indulge with a clear conscience knowing that they are an excellent source of vitamins and minerals.

Oysters with toasted sesame seed mayonnaise

Remove 2 dozen rock oysters from their shells and wipe them with a damp cloth to remove any grit. Wash the shells thoroughly. Put the oysters back in their shells, cover with a damp cloth and refrigerate. Add 1 crushed garlic clove, 1 tablespoon sesame oil and 2 tablespoons toasted sesame seeds to 1/3 cup (80 g) whole-egg mayonnaise, and stir well to combine. Season well. Arrange the oysters on a serving platter and top each with a dollop of mayonnaise and a sprig of dill. Serve with lime wedges. *Serves 6*

Mussels in ratatouille

Cover 1 kg scrubbed and debearded black mussels with a damp cloth and refrigerate. (Discard any open ones.) Heat 2 tablespoons olive oil in a pan and cook 1 finely chopped onion and 2 crushed garlic cloves for 5 minutes, or until softened. Dice 2 baby eggplants, 2 zucchini, 1 red and 1 green capsicum, and add to the onion, continuing to cook for 10 minutes. Increase the heat to high and add a 420 g can chopped tomatoes and 1 cup (250 ml) red wine. Bring to the boil, then reduce the heat and simmer for 30 minutes. Add the mussels to the sauce and cover with a lid. Shake the pan occasionally for even cooking and remove the mussels as soon as they open to avoid overcooking. This may take 5–10 minutes, though some will open a lot quicker than others. Discard any that do not open. Remove the lid and stir until the sauce has thickened slightly. Spoon the sauce over the mussels and sprinkle liberally with 1/4 cup (7 g) chopped fresh flat-leaf parsley. *Serves 6*

Scallops with honeydew and mint chutney

Remove 2 dozen scallops from their shells, clean with a damp cloth, and wash the shells. Put the scallops in a bowl with the juice of 2 limes, cover and refrigerate. To make the chutney, combine 1 tablespoon white wine vinegar, 1 tablespoon finely chopped fresh mint, 2 tablespoons toasted flaked coconut and ½ cup finely diced honeydew melon. Cook the scallops on a char-grill or barbecue plate for 1–2 minutes each side, or until just tender. Put them back into the cleaned shells and top with a generous spoonful of the chutney. Serve warm or at room temperature. *Serves 6*

Left to right: Oysters with toasted sesame seed mayonnaise; Mussels in ratatouille; Scallops with honeydew and mint chutney; Barbecued prawns with sweet cucumber vinegar; Herbed scampi with butter and sweet cider sauce.

Barbecued prawns with sweet cucumber vinegar

Cook 24 raw prawns in their shells on a char-grill or barbecue plate over medium heat for 1–2 minutes on each side, or until pink. Remove from the heat and cover. Combine ¼ cup (60 ml) white wine vinegar and ⅓ cup (90 g) caster sugar in a pan and bring to the boil. Stir and remove from the heat. Allow to cool. Add 2 tablespoons lime juice, 2 tablespoons fish sauce, 1 seeded, thinly sliced, long red chilli, 1 seeded, thinly sliced, long green chilli, 2 diagonally sliced spring onions, 1 Lebanese cucumber, peeled, halved, seeded and thinly sliced, and ¼ cup (15 g) chopped fresh coriander. Combine well and pour over the cooked prawns. Serve warm. *Serves 4–6*

Herbed scampi with butter and sweet cider sauce

Twist and remove the heads from 12 scampi or langoustines. Cut the scampi in half lengthways. Combine ¼ cup (60 ml) olive oil, the juice of 2 lemons, 2 crushed garlic cloves, ½ cup (15 g) firmly packed finely chopped fresh flat-leaf parsley and ½ cup (30 g) finely chopped fresh dill and pour over the scampi. Cover and refrigerate for at least 1 hour. Cook the scampi, shell-side-down, on a char-grill or barbecue plate for 2 minutes. Turn and cook for a further 2 minutes, or until tender. Meanwhile, simmer ¼ cup (60 ml) alcoholic cider until it has reduced by two-thirds. Lower the temperature and add 25 g butter, stirring until melted. Remove from the heat and pour over the scampi. Serve immediately. *Serves 6*

BAKED RICOTTA

Preparation time: 15 minutes +
  overnight draining
Total cooking time: 30 minutes
Serves 8–10 as an appetiser

1 whole fresh ricotta (2 kg)
3/4 cup (185 ml) olive oil
3/4 cup (185 ml) lemon juice
2 tablespoons julienned lemon rind
2 cloves garlic, crushed
1/2 cup (20 g) fresh basil leaves,
  finely shredded
1/2 cup (50 g) semi-dried tomatoes,
  roughly chopped

1 Put the ricotta in a plastic colander, place over a bowl, cover with plastic wrap and leave to drain in the refrigerator overnight.

2 Preheat the oven to very hot 250°C (500°F/Gas 10). Line a baking tray with baking paper. Place the ricotta on the tray and brush with a little of the olive oil. Cook in the oven for 30 minutes, or until golden brown. Allow to cool slightly.

3 Place the olive oil, lemon juice and rind, garlic and basil in a bowl. Mix well and season to taste with salt and pepper.

4 Place the whole ricotta on a serving platter, pour on the dressing and scatter with the semi-dried tomatoes.

Serve with thin slices of Italian-style bread or bruschetta.

NUTRITION PER SERVE (10)
Protein 20 g; Fat 40 g; Carbohydrate 3.5 g; Dietary Fibre 0 g; Cholesterol 95 mg; 1917 kJ (458 cal)

NOTE: If your ricotta comes in a basket, it may have a piece of paper in the base. Make sure you remove this before draining.

Bake the ricotta in a very hot oven until it is golden brown.

Combine all the dressing ingredients and season well with salt and black pepper.

SPICY NUTS

Preparation time: 10 minutes +
  cooling
Total cooking time: 20 minutes
<u>Serves</u> 6

2 tablespoons olive oil
1/2 teaspoon ground cumin
1/2 teaspoon ground coriander
1/2 teaspoon garlic powder
1/4 teaspoon chilli powder
1/4 teaspoon ground ginger
1/4 teaspoon ground cinnamon
2/3 cup (65 g) pecans
2/3 cup (100 g) raw cashews
1 1/2 cups (235 g) raw almonds

1 Preheat the oven to slow 150°C (300°F/Gas 2). Heat the olive oil in a heavy-based pan and add the spices. Reduce the heat to low and cook, stirring constantly, for 5 minutes, or until the spices are fragrant. Remove the pan from the heat and add the nuts. Stir well with a wooden spoon until the nuts are well coated with the spice mixture.

2 Spread the mixed nuts over a large oven tray and bake for 15 minutes, or until golden. Sprinkle the nuts with salt and leave to cool in the oven tray for 10 minutes.

NUTRITION PER SERVE
Protein 12 g; Fat 45 g; Carbohydrate 5 g; Dietary Fibre 5.5 g; Cholesterol 0 mg; 1919 kJ (458 cal)

NOTE: Spicy nuts can be kept in an airtight container for up to 10 days.

Stir the nuts through the spice mixture until they are well coated.

Bake the coated nuts in a large oven tray until they are golden.

WARM DRINKS

Steaming hot chocolate drinks, mulled wine and hot toddies bring out the Christmas traditionalist in us all. What an ideal way to warm the body and the soul!

Chocolate hazelnut drink

Place 2 cups (500 ml) milk, ¼ cup (80 g) chocolate hazelnut spread and 50 g finely chopped dark chocolate in a pan and heat slowly, without boiling. Stir constantly for 5 minutes, or until the chocolate has melted. Divide between 2 mugs and top with whipped cream and roughly chopped roasted hazelnuts. *Serves 2*

Brandied apple cider

Thinly slice an apple into discs, discarding the ends—do not core. Place the apple in a large heavy-based pan and add 1 bottle (375 ml) alcoholic cider and ½ cup (125 ml) brandy or Calvados. Heat until almost boiling—do not boil. Serve in heatproof glasses. *Serves 2*

Hot toddy

Put 2 teaspoons soft brown sugar, 2 slices of lemon, 2 cinnamon sticks, 6 whole cloves, ¼ cup (60 ml) whisky and 2 cups (500 ml) boiling water in a heatproof jug. Stir to combine and leave to infuse for a few minutes, then strain through a sieve. Add more sugar, if desired. *Serves 2*

Left to right: Chocolate hazelnut drink;
Brandied apple cider; Hot toddy;
Hot buttered rum; Hot caramel and
vanilla milkshake; Mulled wine.

Hot buttered rum

Place 2 teaspoons sugar, ½ cup
(125 ml) rum and 1 cup (250 ml)
boiling water in a heatproof jug.
Stir to dissolve the sugar, then
divide between 2 mugs. Stir
1–2 teaspoons softened unsalted
butter into each mug and serve.
Serves 2

Hot caramel and vanilla milkshake

Slowly heat 2 cups (500 ml)
milk in a pan—be careful not
to boil. Add 50 g hard caramels
and heat until melted, stirring
occasionally. Place in a blender
with 1–2 scoops vanilla ice
cream, and blend briefly until
smooth. Pour the mixture into
2 tall glasses. *Serves 2*

Mulled wine

Stick 12 cloves into 2 oranges
and place in a pan with ¼ cup
(60 g) sugar, ½–1 whole nutmeg,
grated, 4 cinnamon sticks and
2 sliced lemons. Add 2 cups
(500 ml) water and bring to
the boil, then reduce the heat
and simmer for 20 minutes. Cool,
then strain. Place the mixture
in a pan and add 3 cups (750 ml)
full-bodied red wine and heat
until almost boiling—do not boil
or the alcohol will evaporate off.
Serve in heatproof glasses. *Serves 6*

CHILLED DRINKS

To set the party mood, the look of a cocktail is almost as important as the taste. Serve strong alcoholic drinks in small tumblers or glasses, and mixed and non-alcoholic drinks in goblets or highball glasses.

Pineapple crush

Peel and cube a fresh pineapple and place it in a blender with 2 cups (270 g) crushed ice. Blend until smooth and then add to a bowl with 1 litre ginger beer and stir to mix. Serve with a fresh piece of pineapple for garnish. *Serves 4*

Frozen passionfruit margarita

Put 80 ml tequila, 30 ml Cointreau, 40 ml lime juice and the sieved pulp and juice of 6 passionfruit in a blender with 1 cup (135 g) crushed ice in a blender and whizz together. Dip the rim of 2 glasses in lemon juice and salt, then pour in the margarita. Garnish with lime slices. *Serves 2*

Peach cup

Cut 2 ripe peaches in half, remove the stones and slice thinly. Put these in a bowl with 1 bottle (750 ml) peach brandy, 750 ml peach juice, 1 bottle sparkling rosé and 1 bottle soda water. Stir together and serve garnished with mint sprigs. *Serves 12*

*Left to right: Pineapple crush,
Frozen passionfruit margarita;
Peach cup; Strawberry Champagne punch;
Watermelon cooler, Mint julep.*

Strawberry Champagne punch

Hull and slice 250 g strawberries and place them in a punch bowl. Add 50 g caster sugar, 1/2 cup (125 ml) Grand Marnier or Cointreau and 30 ml Grenadine and leave to stand. Just before serving, add 2 bottles chilled Champagne and 1 bottle soda water. *Serves 12*

Watermelon cooler

Cut 1/2 large or 1 small watermelon into pieces and remove the seeds. Put in a blender with 1–2 cm fresh ginger and 1 cup (250 ml) orange juice and blend until smooth. Pour over crushed ice to serve. (For a decorative effect, cut a slice off the top of the watermelon and scoop out the inside, and use this as a serving bowl for the finished drink.) Serve in highball glasses. *Serves 4*

Mint julep

Place the rind of 3 lemons in a pan with 1 cup (250 g) sugar and 1 cup (250 ml) water. Dissolve the sugar slowly and bring to the boil. Reduce the heat and simmer for 5 minutes, then strain and leave to cool. Juice the lemons, as well as another 2 lemons. Place 4 cups (540 g) crushed ice and 1 cup (20 g) mint leaves in a food processor and whizz briefly to crush the mint. Tip into a large chilled bowl and add the lemon syrup, lemon juice and 1/2 cup (125 ml) whisky. Dip the rims of martini glasses in lemon juice and sugar, pour in the julep and garnish with mint sprigs. *Serves 8–10*

GIFTS AND SWEETS

HANDMADE JAMS, sweets and biscuits are personal gifts which no store-bought presents can ever match. They're practical, cost-effective, individual and come from the heart. You can always make a few more for those unexpected guests who arrive on the doorstep, gift in hand. And as for the gingerbread house—such design, such engineering— who could fail to be impressed?

PINEAPPLE AND MANGO JAM

Preparation time: 30 minutes
Total cooking time: 40 minutes
Makes 1 litre

1 ripe pineapple
2 large mangoes
1 teaspoon grated lemon rind
1/3 cup (80 ml) lemon juice,
    reserving the pips and rind of
    1 lemon
1.2 kg sugar, warmed (see Note)

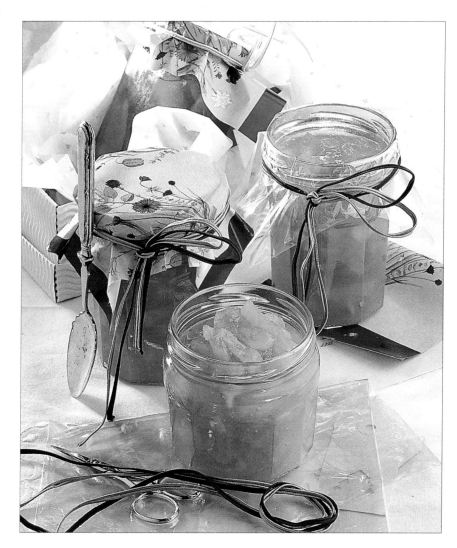

1 Place two plates in the freezer. Remove the skin and the tough eyes from the pineapple. Cut into quarters lengthways, remove the core and cut the flesh into 1 cm pieces. Peel the mangoes and cut each mango cheek from the stone. Cut into 1 cm pieces. Place the pineapple, mango, any juices, lemon rind and juice, and sugar in a large pan. Stir until all the sugar has dissolved.

2 Place the reserved pips and skin onto a square of muslin and tie securely with string. Add to the pan.

3 Bring to the boil, then reduce the heat and simmer, stirring, for 30–40 minutes, or until setting point is reached. Remove any scum with a skimmer or slotted spoon. Stir across the base of the pan to check that the jam is not sticking or burning. Be careful, the jam will froth. When the jam falls from a tilted wooden spoon in thick sheets without dripping, start testing for setting point.

4 Remove from the heat and test for setting point by placing a little jam on one of the plates. A skin will form on the surface and the jam will wrinkle when pushed with your finger when setting point is reached. Remove any scum from the surface.

5 Pour into clean, warm jars and seal. Turn the jars upside down for 2 minutes, then invert and cool. Label and date. Store in a cool, dark place for 6–12 months. Refrigerate after opening for 6 weeks.

NUTRITION PER TABLESPOON
Protein 0.5 g; Fat 0 g; Carbohydrate 30 g; Dietary Fibre 1 g; Cholesterol 0 mg; 497 kJ (120 cal)

NOTE: To warm the sugar, place it in a baking tray in a slow oven (150°C/300°F/Gas 2) for 10–15 minutes, or until warmed through. Warming the sugar speeds up the cooking process.

Simmer until setting point is reached, stirring occasionally to prevent burning.

Setting point is reached when the jam wrinkles when pushed with your finger.

Remove any scum from the surface before pouring the jam into clean, warm jars.

PASSIONFRUIT CURD

Preparation time: 15 minutes
Total cooking time: 20 minutes
Makes 3 cups (750 ml)

4 eggs
3/4 cup (185 g) caster sugar
1/3 cup (80 ml) lemon juice

3 teaspoons finely grated lemon rind
1/2 cup (125 g) passionfruit pulp
200 g unsalted butter, chopped

1 Beat the eggs well, then strain into a heatproof bowl and stir in the remaining ingredients.

2 Place the bowl over a pan of simmering water and stir with a wooden spoon for 15–20 minutes, or until the butter has melted and the mixture coats the back of the spoon.

3 Transfer the curd to a heatproof jug and pour into clean, warm jars.

Seal while hot. Turn the jars upside down for 2 minutes, invert and leave to cool, then refrigerate. Store in the refrigerator for up to 2 weeks.

NUTRITION PER TABLESPOON
Protein 1 g; Fat 5 g; Carbohydrate 5.5 g; Dietary Fibre 0.5 g; Cholesterol 35 mg; 293 kJ (70 cal)

NOTE: For a quick and delicious dessert, fill ready-made tartlet shells with the passionfruit curd and serve with whipped cream.

Strain the beaten eggs into a heatproof bowl before adding the rest of the ingredients.

Stir the mixture constantly until it thickly coats the back of a wooden spoon.

Carefully pour the curd into clean, warm jars and seal while hot.

WHITE CHRISTMAS

Preparation time: 15 minutes +
    30 minutes refrigeration
Total cooking time: 5 minutes
Makes 24

1½ cups (45 g) puffed rice
1 cup (100 g) milk powder
1 cup (125 g) icing sugar

1 cup (90 g) desiccated coconut
⅓ cup (80 g) chopped red
    glacé cherries
⅓ cup (80 g) chopped green
    glacé cherries
⅓ cup (40 g) sultanas
250 g white vegetable shortening
    (copha)

1 Line a shallow 28 x 18 cm tin with foil.

2 Combine the puffed rice, milk powder, sugar, coconut, glacé cherries and sultanas in a large mixing bowl. Make a well in the centre.

3 Melt the shortening over low heat, cool slightly and add to the dry ingredients. Stir the mixture with a wooden spoon until all ingredients are moistened and well combined.

4 Spoon into the prepared tin and smooth down the surface with wetted hands or the back of a spoon. Refrigerate for 30 minutes, or until set. Cut into small triangles to serve.

NUTRITION PER PIECE
Protein 1.5 g; Fat 14 g; Carbohydrate 14 g; Dietary Fibre 0.5 g; Cholesterol 4.5 mg; 775 kJ (185 cal)

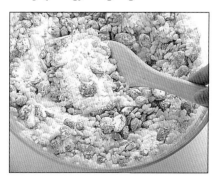

Combine all the dry ingredients in a bowl before adding the melted shortening.

Once the ingredients are moistened, spoon into the tin and smooth the surface.

When the mixture has set, cut it into small triangles to serve.

PANFORTE

Preparation time: 30 minutes
Total cooking time: 1 hour
Serves 10–12

edible rice paper
1/2 cup (60 g) walnuts
3/4 cup (115 g) blanched almonds
3/4 cup (105 g) hazelnuts
1/4 cup (45 g) chopped dried figs
150 g glacé mixed peel, chopped
50 g glacé apricots, chopped
2 tablespoons finely grated
    orange rind
2 tablespoons cocoa powder
1/2 cup (60 g) plain flour
1 teaspoon ground cinnamon
1 teaspoon mixed spice
1/2 cup (175 g) honey
1/4 cup (60 g) caster sugar
1 tablespoon plain flour, extra
1/4 teaspoon ground cinnamon,
    extra

1 Preheat the oven to moderate 180°C (350°F/Gas 4). Line the base of a 22 cm round springform tin with rice paper trimmed to fit. Place the walnuts and almonds on a small baking tray and bake for about 8–10 minutes, or until fragrant and lightly toasted. Transfer to a plate to cool, then repeat with the hazelnuts. When cool, tip the hazelnuts onto a clean tea towel and rub vigorously to remove all the loose skin. Roughly chop all the nuts.

2 Combine the nuts, dried figs, glacé mixed peel, glacé apricots and orange rind in a bowl. Sift in the cocoa, flour, spices and 1/4 teaspoon white pepper, stir to combine, then make a well in the centre. Combine the honey and sugar in a pan and stir

over low heat without boiling until the sugar has dissolved.

3 Pour the honey mixture onto the dry ingredients, stirring until well combined. Transfer to the prepared tin and press in firmly. Smooth the surface with a wetted hand. Use a small sieve to dust the surface with the combined extra flour and cinnamon. Bake for 35 minutes, then cool completely in the tin. Serve in thin wedges.

NUTRITION PER SERVE (12)
Protein 6 g; Fat 15 g; Carbohydrate 37 g; Dietary Fibre 4 g; Cholesterol 0 mg; 1255 kJ (299 cal)

NOTE: Glacé citron (which can be used in place of mixed peel) and edible rice paper are available from delicatessens, speciality stores and health food shops. This recipe makes quite a large panforte, ideal for cutting into sections to give as gifts.

Line the base of the springform tin with rice paper trimmed to fit.

Rub the roasted hazelnuts vigorously in a tea towel to remove the loose skin.

Press down on the surface of the mixture with a wetted hand to smooth.

HANDMADE SWEETS

Handmade sweets and chocolates make ideal gifts for unexpected visitors, or decorations for your Christmas table setting.

Sesame caramel toffee

Mix 1 cup (250 g) caster sugar, 90 g butter, 1/2 cup (160 g) sweetened condensed milk, 1/3 cup (80 ml) glucose syrup and 2 tablespoons golden syrup together and cook over low heat, without boiling, until all the sugar has dissolved. Brush the side of the pan with a pastry brush dipped in warm water to prevent crystallisation. Bring to the boil, stirring constantly, and boil for 10 minutes. Stir in 1 cup (155 g) toasted sesame seeds and spread the mixture into a 20 cm square tin which has been coated with a non-stick spray. Cool for 15–20 minutes and turn out of the tin. Cut into finger-length pieces while still warm. *Makes 20*

Crunchy nuts

Preheat the oven to warm 170°C (325°F/Gas 3). Beat 2 egg whites in a dry, clean bowl with a pinch of salt until soft peaks form. Slowly add 1 cup (250 g) caster sugar and beat well until dissolved to form a meringue. Fold 3 1/2 cups (420 g) whole toasted nuts (blanched almonds, hazelnuts, pecans, walnuts, cashews, brazils) and 1 teaspoon cinnamon into the meringue. Melt 125 g butter in a 15 x 10 x 3 cm baking tray. Spread the nut mixture over the butter and bake for 30 minutes, stirring every few minutes, or until the nuts and coating are browned and there is no butter remaining in the pan. Cool and break into pieces. *Makes 3 1/2 cups (420 g)*

Rich almond rum balls

Melt 225 g chopped dark chocolate, then remove from the heat. Add 100 g diced butter and 2 teaspoons rum and beat until smooth. Beat in 175 g icing sugar, then refrigerate the mixture until firm. Shape 2 teaspoons of the mixture into balls with a 2.5 cm diameter. Finely chop 100 g slivered toasted almonds. Lay these out on a sheet of baking paper and roll the balls over them, coating them in almonds. Serve in gold paper cases. *Makes 35*

Left to right: Sesame caramel toffee; Crunchy nuts; Rich almond rum balls; Uncooked chocolate fudge; Lemon coconut truffles; Rich orange truffles.

Uncooked chocolate fudge

Break 225 g milk chocolate melts into small pieces and put into a bowl with 100 g unsalted butter. Place the bowl over a pan of hot water and heat gently until melted. In a separate bowl, beat 1 egg, then gradually add 450 g icing sugar, 1/2 cup (160 g) sweetened condensed milk and, finally, the chocolate mixture. Beat well and put into a lightly buttered 27.5 x 17.5 cm tin. Chill in the refrigerator for 3 hours, or until firm, then cut into squares. Chopped nuts, dried fruit or orange rind can also be added to the fudge. Store in the refrigerator. *Makes 20 squares*

Lemon coconut truffles

Heat 1/4 cup (60 ml) cream and 250 g chopped white chocolate melts in a pan over low heat until the chocolate has just melted. Remove the pan from the heat and stir in 1 tablespoon grated lemon rind, 2 teaspoons lemon juice and 1/2 cup (45 g) desiccated coconut. Leave to cool for 30 minutes, then refrigerate for 1 1/2 hours. Place teaspoonsful of the mixture onto a foil-lined tray and put back in the refrigerator for 45 minutes. Roll into balls and put back in the refrigerator for 10 minutes, then coat with toasted shredded coconut—you will need about 3/4 cup (45 g). Keep refrigerated until ready to serve. *Makes 40*

Rich orange truffles

Combine 50 g chopped unsalted butter and 100 ml cream in a small pan. Heat gently until the butter has melted and the cream is bubbling. Remove from the heat and add 200 g milk chocolate melts, broken into pieces. Stir well until the chocolate melts. Stir in 1 egg yolk, 2 tablespoons finely chopped mixed peel, 2 tablespoons Grand Marnier and 1 teaspoon grated orange rind. Refrigerate for 3 hours, or until firm. Roll into small balls and coat lightly in cocoa powder. Return to the refrigerator until firm. Melt 140 g dark or milk chocolate melts. Using a fork or toothpick, dip each truffle in the chocolate, let the excess drip off and place on a tray lined with baking paper. Refrigerate to set and keep chilled until ready to serve. *Makes 30*

PANETTONE

Preparation time: 30 minutes
  + soaking and rising
Total cooking time: 35 minutes
Makes 8

½ cup (95 g) chopped dried
  apricots
½ cup (75 g) currants
½ cup (60 g) sultanas
½ cup (125 ml) Marsala
2 x 7 g sachets dried yeast
¾ cup (185 ml) warm milk
½ cup (125 g) caster sugar
180 g unsalted butter, softened
2 teaspoons vanilla essence
3 eggs
2 egg yolks
4 cups (500 g) plain flour
1 teaspoon ground aniseed

1 Combine the dried apricots, currants, sultanas and Marsala in a bowl, cover with plastic wrap and leave to stand for 1 hour, or until most of the liquid is absorbed. Put the yeast, milk and 1 teaspoon of the sugar in a bowl and leave in a warm place until foamy.

2 Place the butter, vanilla and the remaining sugar in a bowl and beat with an electric mixer until light and fluffy. Add the eggs and the separated egg yolks one at a time, beating well after each addition.

3 Sift the flour and aniseed into a bowl, make a well in the centre and add the yeast mixture, butter mixture and fruit mixture. Mix with a flat-bladed knife, until the whole mixture forms a soft, sticky dough. Cover and leave in a warm place for 40 minutes, or until doubled in size.

4 Preheat the oven to moderately hot 200°C (400°F/Gas 6). Lightly oil the base and sides of eight ½ cup (125 ml) soufflé dishes. Cut a strip of brown paper long enough to fit around the inside of each dish and tall enough to come 10 cm above the edge. Fold down a cuff about 2 cm deep along the length of each strip. Make diagonal cuts up to the fold line on each strip, approximately 1 cm apart. Fit the strips around the inside of the dishes, pressing the cuts so they sit flat around the bottom edge of the dish.

Cut circles of brown paper using the dish as a guide, place in the base of each dish, and grease the paper.

5 Turn the dough out onto a floured surface and knead for 3 minutes, or until smooth. You will need more flour, up to ½ cup (60 g), and the dough should be soft but not sticky. Divide into eight equal portions and press into the dishes. Cover with a tea towel and place in a warm place for an hour, or until doubled in size.

Bake for 30–35 minutes, or until golden brown and cooked through when tested with a skewer. Remove from the soufflé dishes, leaving the paper attached. Dust with icing sugar, if desired. Serve warm, cold or sliced and toasted.

NUTRITION PER PANETTONE
Protein 13 g; Fat 25 g; Carbohydrate 80 g; Dietary Fibre 5 g; Cholesterol 170 mg; 2610 kJ (625 cal)

Mix the ingredients together with a flat-bladed knife to form a dough.

Divide the dough into eight portions and press into the paper-lined soufflé dishes.

STAINED-GLASS WINDOW BISCUITS

Preparation time: 1 hour +
  15 minutes refrigeration
Total cooking time: 12 minutes
Makes about 20

150 g butter, cubed and
    softened
1/2 cup (60 g) icing sugar
1 egg
1 teaspoon vanilla essence
1/3 cup (40 g) custard powder
2 cups (250 g) plain flour
1/4 cup (30 g) self-raising flour
200 g assorted boiled lollies
beaten egg, to glaze

1 Line 2 baking trays with baking paper. Beat the butter and icing sugar until light and creamy. Add the egg and vanilla and beat until fluffy. Beat in the custard powder. Fold in the combined sifted flours.

2 Turn onto a lightly floured surface and knead until smooth. Roll between 2 sheets of baking paper to a 3 mm thickness. Refrigerate for 15 minutes, or until firm.

3 Preheat the oven to moderately hot 200°C (400°F/Gas 6). Divide the lollies into their different colours and crush each colour separately using a rolling pin. Cut out the dough with a 9.5 cm fluted round cutter. Lay the rounds on the trays and use small cutters to cut various shapes from inside the circles.

4 Glaze the biscuits with the beaten egg and then bake for 5 minutes. Don't let the glaze drip into the cut-out sections or the stained glass will be cloudy. Fill each cut-out section

with a different coloured lolly. Bake the biscuits for 5–6 minutes, or until the lollies melt. Leave for 10 minutes, then cool on a wire rack.

NUTRITION PER BISCUIT
Protein 2 g; Fat 6.5 g; Carbohydrate 22 g; Dietary Fibre 0.5 g; Cholesterol 30 mg; 635 kJ (150 cal)

Keeping the colours separate, finely crush the boiled lollies with a rolling pin.

Use small cutters to cut shapes from each of the biscuits before baking.

Fill the cut-out shapes with the different coloured crushed lollies.

SHORTBREAD BELLS

Preparation time: 30 minutes +
   15 minutes refrigeration
Total cooking time:
   25 minutes
Makes about 40

250 g butter
½ cup (125 g) caster sugar
2 cups (250 g) plain flour
½ cup (90 g) rice flour
1 egg white, lightly beaten
edible gold leaf, optional (see Note)

1 Preheat the oven to warm 160°C (315°F/Gas 2–3). Line two baking trays with baking paper. Place the butter and sugar in a bowl and beat with electric or handheld beaters until light and creamy.

2 Sift the plain flour and rice flour into the butter mixture, and mix together with a flat-bladed knife to make a crumbly dough. Gather the mixture together and then turn out onto a sheet of baking paper and press together gently into a rough ball. Place another sheet of baking paper on top of the dough. Roll the mixture out to a 7 mm thickness.

3 Peel off the top sheet of baking paper and cut shapes from the dough using bell-shaped cutters of varying sizes. Cut out as many biscuits as possible from the first rolling of dough, then gently press the leftovers together, re-roll and cut out more shapes. Lift the bells onto the lined baking tray, place in the refrigerator for 15 minutes, then bake for 20–25 minutes, or until golden underneath. Cool on a wire rack.

4 If you want to use gold leaf, lightly brush the top of the biscuits with egg white and lay a piece of gold leaf on top. Rub gently with your finger to transfer the gold leaf from the tissue paper to the biscuit, and lift the paper away. The gold leaf will not cover the biscuit, rather it will give an abstract, decorative effect.

NUTRITION PER BISCUIT
Protein 1 g; Fat 5 g; Carbohydrate 10 g; Dietary Fibre 0.5 g; Cholesterol 15 mg; 385 kJ (90 cal)

NOTE: Edible gold leaf is available from art supply shops and some cake decorating shops. It is expensive, but the effect is worth it.

Mix the flours into the butter using a flat-bladed knife to make a crumbly dough.

Cut shapes out of the dough using a bell-shaped cutter.

Cover small sections of the cooked biscuits with edible gold leaf.

GINGER PECAN BISCOTTI

Preparation time: 30 minutes
  + cooling
Total cooking time:
  1 hour 20 minutes
Makes about 20

1 cup (100 g) pecans
2 eggs
²/₃ cup (155 g) firmly packed
    soft brown sugar
1 cup (125 g) self-raising flour
¾ cup (90 g) plain flour
100 g glacé ginger, finely chopped

1 Preheat the oven to warm 160°C (315°F/Gas 2–3). Spread the pecans onto an oven tray and bake for about 10–12 minutes, or until fragrant and toasted, making sure they don't burn. Tip the pecans onto a board to cool, then roughly chop. Line the oven tray with baking paper.

2 Put the eggs and sugar in a clean, dry bowl and beat with electric beaters until pale and creamy. Sift the self-raising flour and the plain flour into the bowl, and add the pecans and glacé ginger. Mix to a soft dough, then place onto the prepared tray and shape into a 9 x 23 cm loaf.

3 Bake the loaf for 45 minutes, or until lightly golden. Transfer to a wire rack to cool for 15 minutes on either side, then carefully cut into 1 cm slices with a large serrated bread knife. The biscotti will be crumbly on the edges so work slowly and if possible try to hold the sides as you cut. Arrange the slices in a single layer on baking trays. Bake for about 10 minutes each side. Don't worry if they don't seem fully dry as they will become crisp on cooling. Cool the biscotti completely before storing in an airtight container for 2–3 weeks.

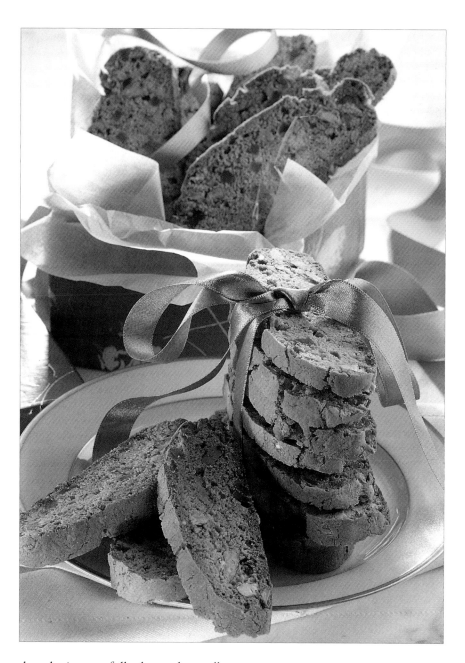

NUTRITION PER BISCUIT
Protein 2.5 g; Fat 4 g; Carbohydrate 20 g; Dietary Fibre 1 g; Cholesterol 18 mg; 530 kJ (125 cal)

Add the nuts and ginger to the mixture and mix to a soft dough.

Place the dough on the prepared baking tray and shape into a log shape.

Using a large serrated bread knife, carefully cut the log into slices.

GINGERBREAD HOUSE

Preparation time: 1 hour
30 minutes + 50 minutes chilling
Total cooking time: 12 minutes per
baking tray
Serves 30

GINGERBREAD
250 g unsalted butter, softened
2/3 cup (125 g) soft brown sugar
1/2 cup (175 m l) golden syrup
2 egg, lightly beaten
4 cups (500 g) plain flour
1/2 cup (60 g) self-raising flour
2 tablespoons ground ginger
2 teaspoons bicarbonate of soda

ICING
50 ml lemon juice
2 cups (250 g) pure icing sugar,
sifted
assorted food colourings
assorted sweets and sprinkles

1 Preheat the oven to moderate 180°C (350°F/Gas 4). Line 4 baking trays with baking paper. Place the butter, sugar and golden syrup in a bowl and beat until light and creamy. Add the eggs gradually, beating thoroughly after each addition. Sift the dry ingredients into the bowl and stir until combined. Bring the dough together with your hands and turn it out onto a well-floured work surface. Knead until the mixture is smooth. Cover the mixture with plastic wrap and refrigerate for 30 minutes.

2 Cut paper patterns for the house. The sides should be 11 x 18 cm, the roof 17 x 22 cm and the front

and back 14 x 24.5 cm. (measure 14.5 cm down from the centre of one of the ends and draw a line across the rectangle, draw a line from the centre point on the end to the point where the line meets each side—this will give you a triangular end to the rectangle, then cut off the corners).

3 Working quickly, divide the mixture into 6 portions and roll each out between two sheets baking paper to a 5 mm thickness. Using the templates as a guide, cut out two roof pieces, two front pieces and two sides of the house. If you would like windows or a door on your house, cut these from the gingerbread. Lift the pieces onto the baking trays and refrigerate for 20 minutes before baking. Bake for 12 minutes each and then leave to cool.

4 To make the icing, place the lemon juice in a bowl and add the icing sugar gradually until you have a smooth mixture which will stay in place when piped—if it is too runny, add more icing sugar. To assemble the house, join the front and sides of the house together with a piped line of icing and leave to dry. Add the back to the house in the same way, hold for a few minutes, then stand up to dry. Decorate the outside seam with more piped icing to strengthen it. Attach the roof pieces using more piped icing. Leave everything to dry before decorating. Attach sweets with icing or pipe decorations such as roof tiles or ivy onto the house.

NUTRITION PER SERVE
Protein 1 g; Fat 7 g; Carbohydrate 19.5 g; Dietary Fibre 0 g; Cholesterol 33 mg; 595 kJ (142 cal)

NOTE: This quantity of gingerbread makes 30 gingerbread men.

Gently bring the gingerbread dough together with your hands.

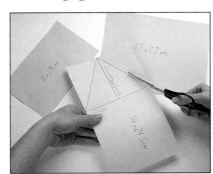

Make paper templates of the house before cutting the dough.

Cut windows and doors out of the gingerbread with cutters.

Mix together the lemon juice and icing sugar to a smooth consistency.

Join the sides of the house together, using piped icing as glue.

Carefully add the roof pieces to the house and leave to dry.

LIQUEUR FRUITS

A perfectly indulgent way to finish off a holiday feast—luscious summer fruits soaked in rich, mouthwatering liqueurs.

Peaches in spiced Sauternes

Halve 4–6 kg ripe slipstone peaches, discard the stone and pack the peaches, along with 1 cinnamon stick and 1 star anise into a clean, warm 2 litre clip-top or preserving jar. Place 2 cups (500 g) sugar in a pan, add 2 cups (500 ml) water and stir over low heat until all the sugar has dissolved. Bring to the boil (at least 85°C) and boil for 5 minutes, then pour the hot syrup over the peaches and top with 1 cup (250 ml) Sauternes. Seal, invert for 2 minutes and store in a cool dry place for 2 weeks. *Fills a 2 litre jar*

Cherries in vanilla brandy

Prick the skins of 750 g cherries with a fine skewer. Heat 1½ cups (375 g) sugar with 100 ml water and 100 ml brandy in a pan, stirring until all the sugar is dissolved. Add the cherries and a vanilla bean and heat until boiling (at least 85°C). Place the cherries, syrup and 200 ml brandy in a clean, warm jar, seal and invert for 2 minutes. Store in a cool, dry place for 6 weeks, turning every couple of days for the first 2 weeks. Serve the fruit in its own liqueur. *Fills a 1 litre jar*

Drunken prunes with vanilla

Place 750 g pitted prunes in a clean, warm 1 litre clip-top or preserving jar. Cut a vanilla bean in half and place in the jar. Add 2 cups (500 ml) tawny port to cover the prunes, seal and invert for 2 minutes. Leave in a cool, dark place for at least 1 month before using. Store for up to 6 months. *Fills a 1 litre jar*

Left to right: Peaches in spiced Sauternes; Cherries in vanilla brandy; Drunken prunes with vanilla; Dried fruit salad with rum; Pears in mulled wine; Dried figs in liqueur muscat.

Dried fruit salad with rum

Place 1 cup (250 g) sugar, ½ cup (125 ml) orange juice, 2 strips orange rind and a vanilla bean in a pan and stir over low heat until all the sugar has dissolved. Bring to the boil (at least 85°C) for 5 minutes, then pour over 600 g of your choice of mixed dried fruits. Stir in ½ cup (125 ml) dark rum. Spoon the fruits into a warm, clean 1 litre clip-top or preserving jar and pour in the syrup. Tap to remove air bubbles, seal and invert for 2 minutes. Leave in a cool, dark place for at least 1 month before using. Store for up to 6 months. *Fills a 1 litre jar*

Pears in mulled wine

Place 2 cups (500 g) sugar and 3 cups (750 ml) red wine in a large pan. Stir over low heat until the sugar has dissolved. Add 1.25 kg peeled, halved and cored small pears, 1 cinnamon stick, 6 whole allspice, 6 cloves and 2 strips each of orange and lemon rind. Cover with a small plate to keep the pears submerged. Bring to the boil (at least 85°C), then reduce the heat and simmer for 10 minutes, or until just tender. Arrange the pears in a warm, clean 1 litre clip-top or preserving jar. Boil the syrup for 15 minutes, then mix ½ cup (125 ml) syrup with ½ cup (125 ml) brandy and 3 cloves. Pour over the pears to cover, seal and invert for 2 minutes. Leave in a cool, dark place for at least 1 month. Store for up to 6 months. *Fills a 1 litre jar*

Dried figs in liqueur muscat

Cut the stalks from 750 g dried figs and place in a non-metallic bowl. Heat 2 cups (500 ml) orange juice and a cinnamon stick in a small pan until just boiling. Pour over the figs and allow to stand for 10 minutes. Drain and reserve the liquid. Place the figs and cinnamon stick in a clean, warm 1 litre clip-top or preserving jar. Heat the reserved liquid to boiling (at least 85°C) and add ¾ cup (185 ml) liqueur muscat. Pour over the figs and tap to remove air bubbles. Add any remaining liquid to cover the fruit, if required, and gently shake to combine. Seal, invert for 2 minutes and leave in a cool, dark place for at least 1 month before using. Top up with liqueur muscat to ensure the fruit is always covered. Store for up to 6 months. *Fills a 1 litre jar*

VINEGARS AND DRESSINGS

Unusually shaped bottles and jars quickly turn these delicious vinegars and dressings into much sought-after gifts. In fact, you may be tempted to keep them all for yourself!

Blueberry and mint vinegar

Place 2 cups (500 ml) white wine vinegar, 2 cups (310 g) fresh or frozen blueberries and 4 fresh mint sprigs in a pan. Bring to the boil, then reduce the heat and simmer for 5 minutes. Remove the mint sprigs and pour the mixture into a clean, warm jar. Add fresh mint sprigs, seal and keep in a cold place for 7 days. Line a funnel with muslin and strain the vinegar into clean, warm bottles. Seal and label. Keep for up to 1 year.
Makes 3 cups (750 ml)

Mint and teriyaki dressing

Put ¼ cup (5 g) fresh mint leaves, 1 tablespoon fresh dill sprigs, ⅓ cup (80 ml) lemon juice, 1 cup (250 ml) apple cider vinegar, 1 teaspoon honey and ½ cup (125 ml) teriyaki sauce in a food processor, and combine well. Season. Keep refrigerated for 1 week.
Makes 2 cups (500 ml)

Yoghurt and anchovy dressing

Put 800 g plain yoghurt, 180 g drained anchovy fillets and 2 teaspoons lemon juice in a food processor and combine well. Season to taste with black pepper and store in the refrigerator for up to 3 days.
Makes 3 cups (750 ml)

Left to right: Blueberry and mint vinegar; Mint and teriyaki dressing; Yoghurt and anchovy dressing; Lemon, lime and thyme vinegar; Peach and basil vinegar; Sweet orange and parsley dressing.

Lemon, lime and thyme vinegar

Put the juice and rind from 2 lemons and 2 limes in a pan with 1 litre white wine vinegar and 10 fresh thyme sprigs and bring to the boil. Reduce the heat and simmer for 5 minutes. Remove from the heat and stand at room temperature until cold. Meanwhile, place the rind of another 2 lemons in a clean, warm jar and add 10 thyme sprigs. Strain the vinegar and pour it into the jar. Seal and keep in a cool place for 7 days. Line a funnel with muslin and strain the vinegar into clean, warm bottles. Add the lime leaves, seal and label. Keep for up to 1 year. *Makes l litre*

Peach and basil vinegar

Place 2 cups (430 g) drained canned peach slices, 1 cup (250 ml) white wine vinegar and 1 cup (60 g) fresh basil leaves in a pan. Bring to the boil, then reduce the heat and simmer for 5 minutes. Remove from the heat and stand at room temperature until cold. Meanwhile, put 1 cup (60 g) fresh basil leaves in a clean, warm jar. Remove the peach slices and basil leaves from the vinegar and pour the liquid into the jar. Seal and keep in a cool place for 7 days. Line a funnel with muslin and strain the vinegar into clean, warm bottles, seal and label. Keep for up to 1 year. *Makes 1¾ cups (440 ml)*

Sweet orange and parsley dressing

Combine 2 tablespoons white vinegar, 2 tablespoons cider vinegar and 2 tablespoons red wine vinegar with 2 tablespoons lemon juice. Add 1 teaspoon salt and whisk until dissolved. Slightly heat 1 cup (250 ml) orange juice with 2 tablespoons honey and stir. Pour over the vinegar mixture and add 3 tablespoons Dijon mustard, 2 tablespoons drained and finely chopped capers, 2 diced sweet gherkins, 4 tablespoons chopped fresh flat-leaf parsley and ½ cup (125 ml) olive oil. Season to taste with ground black pepper. This dressing may be served either warm or cold. Keep refrigerated for 1 week. *Makes 2½ cups (600 ml)*

HINTS AND TIPS

❋ If your attempts to roast a turkey or bake a ham are a one-off and your budget is tight, buy disposable foil baking dishes from supermarkets. Be careful though, they can bend with too much weight which can be hazardous when hot. Use two together to help strengthen the dishes under the weight of your turkey or ham.

❋ You will need plenty of fridge space for a large turkey or ham. This may require removing a shelf and some organisation to fit.

❋ Don't leave foods unrefrigerated for too long in warmer climates or heated rooms. Room temperature is the perfect environment for bacteria to breed. This can cause food poisoning, especially in chicken, duck and turkey.

❋ Think about what else you need to be cooking in the oven at the same time as your roast. For example, how are you going to fit the roast vegetables in the oven if they are being served alongside the ham? A covered kettle barbecue is ideal for cooking hams, allowing you a lot more space in your oven on the day.

❋ Don't fret if you have leftovers—you don't have to eat ham sandwiches for a week. Turkey and ham leftovers can be turned into a variety of tasty dishes. See pages 40–43 for some great ideas!

❋ It is worth paying extra for good-quality dried and glacé fruits for your cake or pudding. Look for plump, moist and glossy fruit which will help prevent your baked goods from drying out and improve the overall flavour. Soaking the fruits for two days prior to baking also enhances both flavour and moistness. For those who like their cake a little on the tipsy side, make the cake at least a few weeks ahead, and then once a week prick the top of the cake with a needle or very thin cake skewer and carefully spoon over a little alcohol of your choice (usually brandy), letting it soak in. Make sure you re-wrap it well each time.

❋ If you are making a boiled pudding, don't forget to buy some calico and string and make sure you have a pot large enough to boil it in.

❋ Christmas cakes and puddings make great gifts too, and look wonderful when packaged either with colourful wrappings or simply some brown paper, straw and a couple of holly leaves.

❋ Make ice cubes from fruit juices for additional festive colour and flavour in your drinks.

❋ Christmas is a time for people dropping in. You will save money and stress if you have some goodies on hand, such as slices, biscuits, nuts, cake or chocolates. If you are making gifts of jams or vinegars, make a couple of extra jars for those unexpected guests who arrive with a present.

INDEX

INTERNATIONAL GLOSSARY OF INGREDIENTS

capsicum	red or green pepper	tomato paste (Aus.)	tomato purée, double concentrate (UK)
coriander	cilantro		
eggplant	aubergine	tomato purée (Aus.)	sieved crushed tomatoes/ passata (UK)
English spinach	spinach		
sausage mince	sausage meat	yabbies	freshwater crayfish
thick cream	double cream	zucchini	courgette

Published by Murdoch Books® a division of Murdoch Magazines Pty Limited,
GPO Box 1203, Sydney NSW 1045.

Managing Editor: Rachel Carter **Editor:** Anna Sanders **Concept & Design:** Norman Baptista **Food Director:** Jody Vassallo **Food Editors:** Jane Lawson, Lulu Grimes **Recipe Development:** Roslyn Anderson, Janene Brooks, Rebecca Clancy, Lulu Grimes, Margaret Harris, Kathy Knudsen, Michelle Lawton, Barbara Lowery, Tracey Meharg, Tracy Rutherford, Jody Vassallo, Maria Villegas **Home Economists:** Alison Adams, Laura Ammons, Michelle Lawton, Kerrie Mullins, Kate Murdoch, Justine Poole, Angela Tregonning, Maria Villegas **Nutritionist:** Thérèse Abbey **Photographers:** Craig Cranko, Reg Morrison (steps) **Food Stylist:** Mary Harris **Food Preparation:** Kerrie Mullins, Alison Adams **UK Consultant:** Maggi Altham **Food Technology Liaison Officer, Food Science Australia:** Brigitte Cox **CEO & Publisher:** Anne Wilson **International Sales Director:** Mark Newman.

The nutritional information provided for each recipe does not include any accompaniments, such as rice, unless they are listed in the ingredients. The values are approximations and can be affected by biological and seasonal variations in food, the unknown composition of some manufactured foods and uncertainty in the dietary database. Nutrient data given are derived primarily from the NUTTAB95 database produced by the Australian New Zealand Food Authority.